WHEN THE SON OF MAN COMES

WHEN THE
SON OF MAN
COMES

FEDERICO SUAREZ

Scepter

Contents

1

Faith

Will he find faith on earth?

If the Second Coming of the Son of God suddenly occurred today, in our own time, would the Lord find faith on earth? Our Lord put that very question to his disciples. Saint Luke (18:8) reports it, and it is a little disconcerting, at least on a first reading. The chapter begins with the short parable about the unjust judge who neither feared God nor regarded man and yet ended up giving justice to the persistent widow, just because he wanted to be rid of her. Then Jesus goes on to ask: "And will not God vindicate his elect, who cry to him day and night? Will he delay long over them? I tell you, he will vindicate them speedily." And then, immediately after this, with nothing in between, come these words: "Nevertheless, when the Son of man comes, will he find faith on earth?"

It may be that this last verse is something Jesus said on another occasion and that it was Saint Luke who put it here, after the parable of the unjust judge, but it is also possible that it forms a conclusion to a teaching—that it does follow on from the story about that humble woman who kept begging for justice, despite the judge's indifference, refusing to be discouraged. In any event, it does not matter when Jesus actually posed the question. What I want to look at now is the question itself, because it seems tailor-made for the present state of our world.

Though never to the point of becoming an obsession, it is a question that often echoes in the minds of people who are concerned about the salvation of mankind, especially in circumstances of the sort in which we now-adays find ourselves. What I think is more important, what really causes one to reflect, is the fact that it was Jesus himself who posed the question. If it had been anyone else who asked it, it would at best appeal to the sort of person who likes dealing with hypotheses; it opens up the way to an interesting intellectual exercise. But because it was Jesus who asked it, it is a question that has to be taken very seriously, for God does not toss out this sort of thing just for fun.

Our Lord was not given to inventing hypotheses or devising problems. In fact, he had come to solve problems, and all his preaching is clear, certain, and definite in the sense that it contains no temporizing, doubting, or cavil-ing. People knew what he was saying and why he was saying it. As Saint Paul would put it later, in him there was no yes and no; he was a clear, permanent yes. True, he did speak in parables, and sometimes he was not under-stood. Even now he is not understood, but not because he was not clear and specific: it is simply that our minds are small and sometimes even darkened. This was made very clear to Nicodemus, and yet Nicodemus was a competent, well-educated man, a doctor of the law. There *must* be something behind these words of Jesus, as there is in ev-erything he said; he never spoke superficially.

"But, when the Son of man comes, will he find faith on earth?" Take a look around, and answer the question yourselves. In the final analysis, a Christian is a disciple of Christ, and our Lord put this question to his disciples. However, to answer the question sensibly and not merely intuitively, perhaps we should ask another question first: What did Jesus mean by faith? About what kind of faith was he talking?

The best person to answer this question is Christ him-self. He once restored a blind man's sight, and he did so on the sabbath. This naturally caused a certain hubbub among the Pharisees; they immediately began to cross-examine the man, and eventually he was cast out of the synagogue. Jesus met him afterward and asked him: "'Do you believe in the Son of man?' He answered, 'And who is he, sir, that I may believe in him?' Jesus said to him, 'You have seen him, and it is he who speaks to you.' He said, 'Lord, I believe'" (Jn 9:35–38). This is the kind of faith to which Jesus is referring—believing that he is the Son of God. If someone believes that Jesus is the Son of God, he then believes *in* Jesus; and if he believes in him, then he also *believes* him. Thus faith consists, first, in believing in someone; then, believing someone; and, finally, believing something.

This is because faith is a supernatural gift, a light in one's mind that allows it to see something it could never otherwise have seen because it is dealing with things that are above its natural capacity. But it is a light that, once a man has it, also shows up something that reason could come to know unaided.

I doubt very much whether the times we live in could be described as an age of faith. It would be easier—and probably more correct—to describe them as times of credulity and even of superstition. I don't think it is an exaggeration to describe them like that, for skepticism and agnosticism are not, properly speaking, human attitudes at all, even when assumed under the guise of being a "radical stance." In fact, one never really comes across perfect skepticism or perfect agnosticism. No person ever really doubts absolutely everything or believes in or knows absolutely nothing.

I don't know whether many of you have read Chesterton (my impression is that he is unknown to most young people today). One of his Father Brown stories has to do with the case of the disappearance of a man from a locked room in a high-rise building that no one enters and no one can leave without being seen—yet, despite this, a little later on, the man is found hanging in a public park near the building in question. Three materialists, after discussing all the possible explanations, eventually convince themselves that the only explanation is some kind of spiritual intervention, perhaps even some supernatural intervention, whereas the whole affair has a natural, and even very simple, explanation. And Father Brown, after solving the case, comments: "You all swore that you were hardened materialists, and in spite of that you were ready to believe anything. There are thousands of people around these days who hold the same position as yourselves, but they are all on a very narrow strip with very little room for sitting down. They will not rest at ease until they believe in something."

That is quite true, I think. That is why I say that, when some one—or some age—has no faith in the supernatural, he or it ends up credulous or superstitious. He will not believe in Christ, yet he is ready to believe in anything at all, however little basis there is for it, or in the power to govern man's destiny and human events that the stars are said to possess, or in some other objects or formulas, which again offer no guarantee of truth.

I dare say you are observant people. Have you never noticed the extent to which people are inclined to believe in anything at all whenever their faith decreases or weakens? Of course, I am referring to people who retain some depth, because superficial people, people who just nibble at things (really they vegetate, rather than live), are so cushioned by their own comfort-seeking tendency and selfishness that they seem more like things than people. You constantly come across types like this in movies and novels and, of course, in the theater. And, unfortunately, too often you find them also among Catholics. However, as long as the soul retains a spark of sensitivity, as long as the person does not refuse absolutely to go to the nub of the question, then the situation is different. In your soul you have to hold on desperately to something with all your strength in order to avoid being completely empty. I remember very well, after the Nanterre student riots in France, seeing a newspaper photograph of a well-known philosopher, then quite an old man, going around Paris selling copies of Dostoyevski's *The Idiot*, sulking like a child because the police hadn't arrested him. They didn't take him seriously. What is left to a man who believes in nothing (except, perhaps, his own theories) but who, perhaps for that very reason, seizes hold of any cause, like a shipwrecked man, if they take away his cause?

There are many people today who do not believe in Jesus Christ, the Son of the living God, but who believe in science, in sociology, in alienation, in economics, in the Marxist analysis of society, in the usefulness of drugs to find oneself or to enter into communion with the universe, in situation ethics; they believe in amazing and incredible theories to "prove" that the miracles of the Gospel are mere symbols (not facts), that virginity is unnatural, that the dogmas defined in the Church are no longer valid, no longer suited to the circumstances and mentality of modern man. There are people who have no faith in Christ, yet they believe these (and other) things.

And what about superstition? If you keep your eyes open you will notice something that is also very symptomatic—the utter illogic of people. On the one hand, they are intent on demythologizing mysteries; yet yet there is a proliferation of astrologers and seers and fortune-tellers. It is amazing (at least it amazes me) to read in *L'Express* that there are more than a thousand registered astrologers in Paris (another publication gave a much larger figure) and in France as a whole almost fifty thousand consulting rooms of witches, soothsayers, and palmists; in Italy, twelve thousand practitioners of occult sciences have formed a trade union; a German astrologer advises major companies on personnel recruitment; an English astrologer has more than a hundred companies as clients, national and international. Referring to young people who consult him, an American astrologer is quoted as saying: "These people are looking for God, and they are afraid of the chaos they find in the world today." Seventy percent of French people regularly read "the Stars and you" columns of the newspapers. The same thing happens all over the world: just look at your daily newspaper or at any newsstand.

You know very well, of course, that faith means believing on the testimony of someone else. And I must tell you that, absolutely speaking, everyone—even atheists, skeptics, Marxists, and scientists—lives on faith. Not on supernatural faith, but on human faith. No one can prove that God does not exist, but an atheist *believes* that he does not exist. If you just reflect about the things you know—not from experience or evidence or working it out logically, but because other people have told you—you will be surprised to find that the greater part of what you are sure of you know on faith. If you know of Napoleon or Socrates, it is through the testimony of other people; if you accept the existence of genes in chromosomes (and, of course, in the existence of chromosomes), it is because someone has told you about them, and you believe that they exist. If Marxists hold the dogmas of class struggle as the moving force of history, of the classless society as the final stage (why final?—will the world end then?) of mankind, they do so by human faith (not even scientific faith) in Marx's word, but not because these statements are "scientifically" proven. In fact, they are improbable or, rather, unprovable. How can you prove the theory of the classless society or the final stage, and so on? Most people who know that blood circulates through the body always at a constant temperature know it on pure faith. How many have ever personally proved it?

Well, then, is it any easier to believe in these things than to believe in Jesus Christ, true God and true man, the only-begotten Son of the Father? Apparently it is, but don't be too surprised at that.

Jesus was not an idealist or a dreamer. On the contrary, he showed so often that he had his feet on the ground that I doubt if there was ever anyone as realistic as he. You can observe this in a number of instances, and the more deeply you read the Gospel the more apparent this realism of Jesus becomes. No, he was not a dreamer or an idealist. The Pharisees, for example, were dreamers and idealists: they imagined an earthly Messiah who was going to turn a small people, Israel, into a great nation governing the whole world, imposing its law on all other nations (the non-chosen peoples) who would have to behave as its pupils; and the Pharisees expected that everything they imagined would come true.

In chapter five of Saint John's Gospel is a statement that shows how clearly Jesus knew the ground he was on and that he was under no illusions: "I have come in my Father's name, and you do not receive me; if another comes in his own name, him you will receive" (Jn 5: 43). Apparently, Jesus was far from thinking that his teaching—it is not quite right to call it "his," because he himself said that he spoke only those things he had heard from his Father—was going to be automatically accepted by people because it was intrinsically good, because it was an expression of the truth. In fact he knew—and he said so—that others would come with far fewer guarantees of speaking the truth, with far fewer proofs of their mission to teach, and their words would be taken up much more readily.

Well, I might now ask you: who or what is this entity people call "modern man"? Look at the proliferation of groups, sects, pseudo-religions, all kinds of heterodox movements—ranging from occasional concerts where the crowds go ecstatic over pop music and enjoy a few days' sense of solidarity in some vague sort of community to the loners, or almost loners, uprooted from a civilization they find oppressive and meaningless, who take off to India or Nepal in the hope of finding themselves again through silence and solitude. Notice how they feel impelled to escape the dryness of a technological and materialistic civilization and lay hold of any kind of esoteric doctrine that will give them back the sense of mystery, anything at all that has soul, anything that cannot be weighed or measured or turned to some "practical" use; something, anything, so long as it speaks to them of what is beyond this material world of ours and gives them even a little bit of horizon and hope—Yoga, Zen Buddhism, even voodoo and magic (black and white)—to fill the gap left by the rejection of faith in Christ: anything, but something, even what is devilish, that rushes to fill the vacuum left by the expulsion of God, of a God become man to save men.

But you are not in this position. You have been given the gift of faith, when you were baptized. And what have you done with it?

The Epistle to the Hebrews (11:6) says: "Without faith it is impossible to please God." Probably some people will find this bald statement quite shocking—people who claim that they are in good faith, although believing whatever they feel like believing and avoiding any kind of renunciation involved in the search for the

kingdom of heaven; and people who have devoted themselves to building an earthly paradise and are bent on
erasing even the very name of Jesus Christ. Yet, without
faith it is impossible to please God. Decide for yourselves: God, out of love for mankind, humbled himself
to the extent of becoming man. As you well know (unless the persistent campaign of de-Christianization has
brainwashed you) the Word became flesh in the womb
of the blessed Virgin, was born in Bethlehem in Judea,
lived among us, suffered death under Pontius Pilate, was
crucified, died, and was buried, rose from the dead and
showed himself to his disciples, and lives in the unity of
the Father and of the Holy Spirit. And he did all this to
show us something that mankind, blind as a bat, disorientated and storm-tossed, was simply unable to see. How
could one possibly please God if, after his taking all this
trouble, we corral him into the modest role of a poor
man who has all sorts of altruistic good feelings but goes
overboard whenever he claims to be the Son of God, God
himself; if we turn him into a good person, no better and
no worse than Buddha, Confucius, or Socrates, who are
also good persons.

New interpretations are being devised every day. There
is a whole array of new masters, all concerned about
man's welfare, all devising solutions for man's problems
and offering them to anyone who will accept them. They
wear themselves out publishing all types of highly complicated surveys, with answers already programmed; they
theorize about the fate of Christianity, deny their religion,
desacralize the sacred, trivialize mystery, pontificate on
what is moral and what is immoral, decide on what is sin
and what is merely taboo. They pronounce ambiguous
and often pedantic statements, which at first sight seem to
be sound and almost self-evident, for example, "the word
of God cannot be grasped by any human word used to

express it"—false phrases, which are accepted and re-
peated and promoted with such enthusiasm and super-
ficiality: the secularization process, the autonomy of the
world, the maturity of mankind, a secular interpretation
of Christianity, and so on.

The "thinkers" in fashion nowadays are really simply
essayists, writing about the ideas that are in fashion.
They shake ideas in their head in the same way as a
barman mixes a cocktail, in the hope that maybe they
will come up with some answer to all these questions—
questions no one can avoid asking if he keeps his mind
alive: What is the meaning of the world and of man?
What is there after death? All the cocktail does is in-
crease the confusion: it exhausts those who really do
want to think. The same kind of thing happened when I
was a student, but those ideas, those philosophers, are
long since forgotten. They had no truths to tell us; they
had only a few ideas that seemed clever at the time but
came to nothing.

No: faith is not evasion. People who like to theorize
enjoy saying that it *is*, but, when you know something for
sure, there is no room for theories. Evasion means escape
from real life in order to submerge yourself in fiction.
Faith does not involve "alienation"—but theories devised
to please us *do*. Recently there was the case of a Nobel
prizewinner, a scientist, who explained the universe by
saying it was "an accident," it just happened. Anything,
even the absurd, rather than allow room for a creative
God.

In any event, the whole question has to do with the
salvation of man.

A brilliant intellectual pirouette might allow one to
flee a problem one doesn't want to face, but that gets one
nowhere (and other people notice it). For others, clever
tricks are not enough; they need to have a real faith. And

then, in a narrow dogmatic nonintellectual way, they latch on to systems, ideologies, and even formulas as stereotyped as television ads, which they trot out as perkily as children who have learned their lesson by heart. People of this sort need to believe in something, because without faith there is no hope. And what kind of a life can a person have if he has no hope? He is in a blind alley.

Banal ideas are being shunted around, enjoying the limelight for a few months, and then being displaced by other equally trivial ideas; the net effect is that people become punch-drunk, anesthetized in the dense chaos created by all those false prophets selling their own wares.

"If I speak the truth, why do you not believe me?" Jesus asked the Pharisees. I would ask you the same question (not that I regard you as Pharisees, of course): If he speaks the truth, why do you not believe him? Of course, because you are so inclined to turn the whole thing into an intellectual exercise, you can turn around and ask me: "And how do I know he is speaking the truth?"

That is a good question, undoubtedly, but are you honorable enough to ask the same question about those in whom you believe and to whose ideas you conform? How do you know that Marx, Hegel, or any other theorist is telling the truth?

As far as Jesus Christ is concerned, I can tell you why I know he spoke the truth: because he rose from the dead. And because from the historical (or, should I say, "scientific") point of view this is much more certain than, for example, the existence of Socrates or any other landmark in ancient history, it is a good basis for believing in Christ; it is what the apologists used to call a "motive of credibility." I defy anyone to show me as firm a basis for lending credit to the theories of some of those who call themselves "theologians"—adult Catholics or modern men—or, while we are at it, dogmatic students of those masters who prophesy utopian paradises or promote values opposed to the Gospel. Personally, I almost feel insulted when I see these great devisers of schemes for the salvation of mankind expecting me to lend them credence without offering me the least guarantee as to why I should believe them.

This is how things stand: as far as concerns belief (for none of his claims is self-evident to human reason) in what Jesus Christ says (Jesus Christ who came and spoke in his Father's name), or in what all those say who have come along and spoken in their own name, the "modern world" and maybe you, or some of you, seem ready to believe, not Jesus Christ who came in his Father's name, but those others who have come in their own name.

And if that *is* the way things are (of course it depends on how right I am), I ask myself, and I would like you to ask yourselves, what are we doing and what are we ready to do—those of us who call ourselves disciples of Christ—so as to bear witness with our lives as the early Christians did with theirs, to Jesus as the Son of God? Because maybe we, like them, can, with their help, bring the joy of hope to a world that has lost it.

2

Obedience

"Not every one who says to me ..."

I suppose you have come across interviews with famous people in which they are asked questions such as: "If your library were on fire and you could save only one book, which one would you choose?"; and in which you always learn some interesting or curious aspect of the person's lifestyle. I have wondered a few times (when I had nothing better to do!) what I would choose out of the Gospels if I were allowed to salvage only two or three verses. In fact, I have never actually come to a satisfactory answer. I don't know what I would choose.

However, if the question were put differently, it might be easy enough. If I were told that I had to choose one short, clear text that would allow people, forever afterward, to have a guideline for choosing between good and evil, a paragraph they could use as an ethical yardstick to guide them and show them how to behave well, then I think I would opt for a few lines from Saint Matthew's Gospel, near the end of the Sermon on the Mount:

> Not every one who says to me, "Lord, Lord," shall enter the kingdom of heaven, but he who does the will of my Father who is in heaven. On that day many will say to me, "Lord, Lord, did we not prophesy in your name, and cast out demons in your name, and do many mighty works in your name?" And then will I declare to them, "I never knew you; depart from me, you evildoers" (Mt 7:21–23).

I daresay you know this text, at least the first few words: the phrase "Not every one who says to me, 'Lord, Lord,'"

19

is often used colloquially. But you have to take the whole text to understand why I think a person could organize his whole life by it.

The passage in question reveals a truth and then gives an example that helps us engrave on our mind and heart the teaching contained therein. The revelation is this: access to the kingdom of heaven is obtained through doing the will of the Father. It is not enough to pay lip service, you actually have to deliver. That is not to say that prayer is a bad thing; it is just not enough. Deeds are also required. And not just any deed: we have to do the will of our Father who is in heaven, the will of God.

This teaching is illustrated in the second part of the text. It would seem that Jesus is referring to the moment of truth, the time of judgment, when some people will boldly claim entrance to the Kingdom of God on the strength of the things they have done in life. And what things! Prophesying, working miracles, casting devils out of possessed people—and not just in any way: they did it in Jesus' name. And here is the thing to notice: whereas you would expect the gates to open wide to let in these highly-qualified people, the gates don't open at all: in fact, God doesn't recognize these people, and he calls them evildoers.

As often happens in the Gospel when Jesus acts or speaks in certain ways, our natural reaction is utter amazement. For is there anything finer than, for example, casting out devils in Jesus' name? And what about prophecy and miracles performed in his name: aren't these sure signs of divine support? How is it, then, that God does not recognize these people and calls them *evil-doers*—as if they had committed sins rather than *praise-worthy actions* done in God's name? Could they have done anything better than what they did?

Of course there is an explanation, but in order to find

it you must understand that Jesus was using this example to illustrate his lesson. He used to do this sort of thing often. You will remember, for example, when the disciples asked him to teach them how to pray and he replied with the Our Father. But then he went on to tell them the story about the friend who goes to his neighbor late at night to ask the loan of the three loaves, and the story of the child asking his father for bread, and so on; I could give you many examples.

What our Lord was trying to make us see is that the will of God is something so important that our very access to heaven depends on it.

And I think that when he says "on that day" he means that a person can do wonderful, marvelous things but if God, in fact, wanted him to do something else, something quite different, even if it was more commonplace and less spectacular, then that person was wasting his time and effort and, sad to say, doing evil. He did evil because, when it came to choosing between God's will and his own, he chose the latter and put it ahead of God's will, which is practically the same as saying that he not only failed to cooperate in carrying out of God's plan, but his arrogance led him to frustrate God's designs. What he did was to prevent God's plans from being fulfilled.

I think you will see this quite easily if you follow my reasoning for a few minutes. Imagine a bank clerk who, during office hours, instead of doing the job he is given, spends his time painting landscapes or writing poems. Painting and poetry are—according to general opinion, anyhow—more noble and loftier activities than adding up long columns of figures. Yet the bank manager is unlikely to reward the clerk for not doing what he was paid to do. There is nothing wrong with playing tennis; in fact, it is very good exercise, and it may be good for the country: the more who play, the more likely that some of us will get somewhere at Wimbledon or Forest Hills or in the Davis Cup. But, even though tennis is good, if someone spends his time at tennis practice when he should be at class (whether he's a teacher or pupil) or in the office or on the building site, then obviously he is not doing anything really good. In fact, I would say he is really doing something bad because he is obviously not doing what he should be doing; he is doing what he should not be doing.

In another sphere altogether you have the classic example (I daresay it never really occurs, at least not in our own times) that used to be given in homilies of the woman who was so devout that she heard Mass two or three times a day, prayed novenas, and did other pious things and left her husband unbreakfasted, the children unwashed, and the house generally in a mess. This woman, we were told, was acting wrongly, even though her going to Mass was good in itself. She was acting wrongly because what God wanted of her, in the first instance, was that she fulfill the duties of her state in life rather than sacrifice them to her personal spiritual preferences. Duty comes before devotion, we might say.

If you think about it a bit you will see that what the Gospel is saying is that obedience is what opens the door to the kingdom of heaven, because only someone who does the will of God, that is, who obeys God, will get in.

I suppose that given the low ratings obedience gets these days—everyone talks about "freedom" and "rights" and "self-determination"—the almost instinctive reaction, especially among young people (who know least), is to ask why must we obey. Not, of course, why one has to obey God (even the least intelligent can answer that question); but why do we have to obey the Church or parents or the government? And here I hesitate to say that we have to obey them because they are the proper channels by which we can discover the will of God, because you will think that is not answer enough. There is a certain tendency today not to accept things unless you find them convincing: the old argument "from authority" doesn't hold as much weight as it used to.

This holds true for most people, and many parents know it to their cost. However, this doesn't mean that young people today do not accept the argument from authority: they do accept it or, at least, their behavior at times implies that they do. They may have many reservations about the authority of the Church or of their parents, but they have no such reservations about the authority of little leaders all over the university or technological college—the people who make up slogans, the smooth talkers who promote modern sexual morality, though I think that this is partly the result of the massification and anonymous character of society.

However, in spite of all that, one thing is certain and clear: either we do God's will or there is no solution, among other reasons because "God desires all men to be saved and to come to the knowledge of the truth," as Saint Paul says to Timothy, and for that result it is necessary to know Jesus Christ and obey him. It is God's will that all men—made from nothing, in his image and likeness—be saved. To save all men, the Son of God became man and died on the Cross, and when he rose from the dead he bore witness to the resurrection of the body and gave us a basis for hope. To show how men could be saved, he gave them the commandments, which are an expression of the natural law, because he was well aware how much people needed help. Can you imagine how much work would be involved if everyone had to reason it out all by himself to reach the basic truths? How many people do you think would ever work them out?

Perhaps that is why, when Jesus was leaving the world, he told his disciples: "Go therefore and make disciples of all nations, baptizing them in the name of the Father and of the Son and of the Holy Spirit, teaching them to observe all that I have commanded you" (Mt 28: 19–20). It is the Church who lets us know the will of God as regards salvation, and we have to obey her instructions because, in things to do with faith and morals, it is she who teaches us to observe all that he has laid down.

I think it would be very good (for those of you who think that way) to give up the idea that the Church orders arbitrary things, just because she feels like it. Let me give you one example of the way young people, in my experience, like to think. When a young person asks why does he have to go to Mass on Sundays when he prefers or gets more devotion from going some other day of the week or not at all; when he thinks along these lines, in addition to showing that he does not trust the Church very much, he shows that, on this score, he is very badly instructed. There is a commandment, the third commandment, which says that we have to keep the sabbath day holy. God was so serious about it that he went to the trouble of laying down a whole series of precise rules about how we had to go about keeping the sabbath day holy. But when the Old law came to an end and the new covenant began with Jesus, Christians from the very beginning, that is, in the lifetime of the Apostles, began to celebrate "the Lord's day." The Lord's Day was Sunday because it was on Sunday that Jesus rose from the dead; and the Lord's day was devoted to celebrating the mysteries, praying, attending the sacrifice of the Mass, and receiving the Body of the Lord in the Eucharist. As time went on, the Church sanctioned this custom, laying it down that Christians should keep Sundays and feast days holy by hearing Mass in full and by abstaining from servile work (the latter rule, with the intention of protecting servants and giving them a certain minimum of rest). Or, as the new Code of Canon Law puts it, "to abstain from such work or business that would inhibit the worship to be given to God, the joy proper to the Lord's day, or the due relaxation of mind and body."

You know that it is a good thing to go to Mass any day, but you are not sanctifying a feast day, simply because there is no feast day to sanctify, and if you do not go to Mass on a Sunday or holy day of obligation you are guilty of grave disobedience to an explicit commandment of God, who wanted you to sanctify that particular day and who, additionally, through the Church, told you how you had to sanctify it (because it is Christ's will that the Church teach us how to observe what he has commanded us). I think that is all very straightforward.

You may think that it is not quite so clear that we have to obey our parents. The fourth commandment says "Honor" your father and mother, not "Obey" your father and mother. Quite correct; I have discussed this elsewhere, so I do not propose to deal with it again here. In any event, so long as we are dependent on our parents there are many points on which we have to obey them. Of course (in my opinion), there are many parents who need to be educated on this score. Imagine, for example, someone who wanted to be a doctor and never managed it because life got in the way; then his great ambition is to see his son become a doctor. He thinks, mistakenly, that what was best for him must be best for his son; whereas his son wants to be a car mechanic, and he is in no way cut out to be a doctor. Here you have a fine way to spoil a life with the best will in the world by arbitrarily failing to respect the boy's freedom or God's will, because the boy doesn't have the talents necessary for medicine. When people give orders where they have only a right to give advice and guidance, the results can be horrendous and sometimes irreparable.

But I doubt that this happens often nowadays. In fact, I'm inclined to think that, far from being too authoritarian, parents nowadays sin by not being authoritarian enough, by not exercising their authority sufficiently. The younger generation does not have much respect for the experience of its elders—and has little or no inclination toward taking their advice. Young people have rejected convention, but they have not substituted principles—they have opted to follow impulses. In spite of all that, the obligation imposed by the fourth commandment still holds good, and it includes to a great extent the obligation to obey our parents as long as we are dependent on them. And parents, for their part, have an obligation to educate their children, which implies very often that they have to order them to do things (because the children do not know what they have to do) or forbid them to do other things (even though they may like doing them). Anyway, you only have to be intellectually honest to understand this. When a young man scarcely past adolescence claims the right to come and go as he pleases and to do whatever he feels like doing, with no restrictions on his timetable or business and no consideration of obedience to his parents, when he wants to be treated like a grown man but is not doing a man's job or accepting a man's responsibility for his actions, then, rather than developing a personality of his own, it is more likely that during his lifetime he will never be more than a capricious spoiled child who has grown up too quickly and turned his whims into a law of his own. Education, the process of becoming a man, is something which necessarily involves obedience—learning, developing habits, self-control—because you cannot have education without obedience. To refuse obedience in order to avoid being different from others is the equivalent, so very often, of being trapped by the conventional modes of behavior of the day. And people who go in this direction run the risk of being ultimately pushed to one side because they are useless or unbearable.

But I don't intend to pursue this line of thought. I simply want to remind you, because you are Catholic Christians, of some words of Saint Paul: "Children, obey your parents in everything, for this pleases the Lord. Fathers, do not provoke your children" (Col 3:20–21). And this also: "Let every person be subject to the governing authorities. For there is no authority except from God, and those that exist have been instituted by God. Therefore he who resists the authorities resists what God has appointed, and those who resist will incur judgment" (Rom 13:1–2). I quote these words just to show you (if I can) that you cannot always expect God to send you an angel with a message to let you know his will. To be certain as to God's will, a Christian has to have faith in revelation, but also he has to use his common sense, he has to reflect a little and be honest enough to play fair rather than trying to convince himself that the right thing is whatever he happens to want to do and that whatever he doesn't like is unjust, arbitrary, and despotic.

It was an act of disobedience resulting from pride (the usual source of disobedience) that brought into the world—which was good when God made it—pain and war, suffering and disease, discord and hatred, selfishness and death. An act of obedience redeemed us all and gave us a chance to be saved, by restoring the original order in a creation that had been thrown out of gear by sin. For if there is no obedience, there is no order, and if there is no order, then all you have is chaos. Saint

Augustine, who, besides being a very intelligent man, experienced the consequences of living a rather disorderly life, said something that was not only profound but true and proven by experience: "Keep order and order will keep you." Order is maintained by obeying a rule, and the supreme rule by which all good is good—for oneself, for others, and for the universe as a whole—is the will of God, to such an extent that an action good in itself but opposed to the will of God becomes something bad and can have disastrous effects—as we can see by those miracle workers whom God called evildoers.

You can be absolutely sure, infinitely surer than if you follow your own ideas (or those of other people, who may have you on a lead), that by obeying those whom God has placed over you with an obligation to command, by obeying in those things in which they have the right to command, you are not only walking on really solid ground but actually pleasing God. A person who does not obey is at the mercy of himself. God help him, because, though he may be sure he is doing his own will, he cannot be sure he is doing what God wants him to do. And he will not be saved by doing his own will.

Of course, there is another question you can raise to give yourselves a way out: What happens if those giving the orders are wrong? I could reply to that with two other questions: And how do you know they are wrong? And what if they are not wrong? But I will answer in another way: If those who have the obligation to give orders *are* wrong, then that is their problem, not yours. They have made a mistake (in the final analysis, men are fallible and can make mistakes), but you will not have gone wrong by obeying. They will have to answer to God for their mistake, if they are guilty of carelessness, self-interest, or arrogance; but if what they have ordered you to do is not a sin—that is, something objectively opposed to God's law, known to us as proposed and taught by the Church—then you *know* that you are not doing wrong by obeying, even though you *think* that their command is wrong.

I daresay all this may sound rather scandalous to some sensitive ears—ears very sensitive to certain things, of course. The word "obedience" in certain sectors is a bad word nowadays; but, in spite of that, it is a word I like, and you also should like it if you still have that quality which allows you rightly to be called Christians. We should like this word, you and I, because if Jesus Christ (the Son of God) "became obedient unto death, even death on a cross" (Phil 2: 8), I think the least we can do is also make an effort to obey, especially if we are not being asked to go that far. He declared that his food was to do the will of him who sent him; for the first thirty years of his life all the Gospel says of him is that "he was obedient to them." He obeyed two human beings, Mary and Joseph, who were infinitely inferior to him and much less intelligent than he was. At the most bitter moment in his life, when he was entering into his Passion and his human nature rebelled against the suffering and humiliation that awaited him even though he was innocent, his own energy was directed to submitting to his Father's plans: "Not my will, but thine, be done" (Lk 22: 42). For he knew that the best thing, the right thing (even for us), is always to do the will of God. This never ceases to amaze me: he accepted an unjust sentence, arrived at in an unjust way, because it was imposed by a legitimate authority and it was the Father's will that he obey legitimate authority. Which he freely did.

So, it is Christ himself, who made his entire life an act of obedience to the Father, who reminds us that we have to do God's will. Not that we have to act as slaves or as employees who agree to work for reward. Reward in this case is not the purpose of obedience; it is only a consequence of it. If obeying is, as Saint Josemaría Escrivá put it, "doing things as God wants, *because we feel like it*, which is the most supernatural of reasons," a Christian will always obey out of love of God: "He who has my commandments and keeps them, he it is who loves me" (Jn 14:21), says Jesus. It seems logical enough, then, to say that if you do not love him, you do not keep his commandments; and also that if you do not keep all of his commandments, then you do not love him, even though God for his part never ceases to love you. Keeping the commandments, obeying God's precepts, is the key to expressing love for God, because love means deeds, not sweet words.

The early Christians had a very good grasp of this idea—that it is not enough to say things; you have to *do* what the Lord commands in order to be properly called his disciples. Thus, Saint Justin, writing in the middle of the second century, was able to say this (many people today may think it harsh): "But let those who are seen not to be living as they ought be declared non-Christians, however much they mouth the teachings of Christ, for he said that those would be saved who not only spoke but who also practiced with deeds."

I confess that those of us who call ourselves Christians and consider ourselves Christians may be made a little uncomfortable by those words. I hope you will find this so if you reflect on them and take a good look at yourselves. Because, in the last analysis, what makes a person really what he professes to be is consistency between the faith he declares and the deeds he actually does. And, apparently, you do not have the right to call yourself a disciple of Christ unless you are resolved to obey his commandments. At least, that is what he himself spells out: "Why do you call me 'Lord, Lord,' and not do what I tell you?" (Lk 6: 46); and Saint Justin says the same thing in his letter to the emperor, without doubt so that he might know how things stood.

To sum up: we can do what we please, and if that is in keeping with what God wanted us to do, wonderful; if not, then we are wasting our time, even if we work miracles.

3

Peace of Soul

"Peace I leave with you."

There can have been few periods of history—if, indeed, any—in which the word "peace' has been more bandied about than our own. To judge from the newspapers, it seems to be a treasure people dream about.

If two countries are at war, there is even more talk about peace, but this does not prevent people from selling arms to the belligerents in order to enable them to keep on fighting. All important speeches deal with peace. Conferences are held about it, reports written, plans made, projects presented to be studied, examined, and discussed and then marked "for further consideration." The members of delegations to peace conferences, their secretaries, advisers, experts, and entourages, speak, argue, propose and counterpropose, exchange notes . . . , and months or years later manage to work out some sort of suitably vague agreement that is generally acceptable. Sometimes no such agreement is reached, and then new conferences have to be scheduled.

And the wars go on, go on in spite of everything, no matter what started them. There is always some reason for every war, and usually the root cause is more complex—and less obvious—than what appears on the surface. Nowadays, governments never even bother to discuss the subject—so popular with the theologians of the sixteenth century—of whether a war is just or not. They have other things to worry about.

After World War II, a supranational organization was

created where states could sort out their differences in a peaceful way, like intelligent, civilized types, full of altruistic ideas and with unlimited faith in the good will of men. The United Nations, an organization endowed with enormous moral authority (that was the idea): How could a country, given that it had voluntarily become a member of the UN and accepted its noble goals, refuse to comply with its decisions? Yet wars have taken place, sometimes even between members of that organization established to promote peace and understanding among nations.

As if that were not bad enough, in many cases the norm is that there is no *internal peace*. There may not be any war, or what is usually understood by "war," but peace certainly is missing. Racial unrest, class struggle, ideological rivalry, party strife. Terrorism, guerrillas, kidnapping, outrages, insecurity, riots, conflict, violence. Hatred, resentment, recrimination.

"Saying 'Peace, peace,' when there is no peace" (Jer 6: 14). What is happening to the world? What is happening to us? Have we not been told—endlessly, euphorically—that mankind has at last come of age? A world that seems to be involved in civil war; nations at loggerheads; a world in whose cities people feel more and more insecure; a world in which conditions (civilization) make people ever more irritable and less friendly: Does that show maturity?

I am afraid that, once again, the theorists have got it all wrong. The fact that man can set up house on the moon, construct electronic brains, invent weapons of amazing precision and destructive power is no reason for his developing a narcissus complex, especially when he looks at other aspects of life, which are nothing to be proud about.

There is no peace in the world; that is quite clear. But

is there even peace in men, peace of soul? So many intense people, with nerves as taut as guitar strings, moving from one place to another in transport that gets faster and faster, people who by the very fact of always being on the move do not even know how to *be* in any place, much less their own home: Are these people who have peace? Are they trying constantly to flee from themselves because they cannot put up with themselves? These cities full of smoke, noise, and asphalt, full of traffic and parked cars, with large honeycomb-looking houses and joyless streets that stretch out into the suburbs, like endless tentacles; these cities which manage to have hundreds and hundreds of thousands of inhabitants and not a single neighbor: Is that a framework which makes for peace among men?

People want peace, countries want peace. And they are right, because without peace, without some sort of peace, at least, life is not worth living. But what kind of peace are they looking for? What is this peace that is so much talked about and written about? The peace of the dead? The peace of those who are under an anesthetic? The mere absence of war? The animal peace someone feels after he has had a good meal?

Or, perhaps, the peace of Christ? The truth is that I am not very sure this expression means anything to many of our contemporaries (Catholics included), and I would even go so far as to say that it means absolutely nothing to those various international organizations or to the people who sit around conference tables trying to work peace out. Sometimes it seems to be just a slogan. At other times it is so *unreal* that there is no place it can be found in the *real* world in which we live, as if it were a kind of dream that can never come true. And, most times, it is just something that sounds good and seems to be the right thing to talk about.

But that is not the way it should be: for Jesus said, "Peace I leave with you; my peace I give to you" (Jn 14:27), and he said this not as something to do with the future but as a gift here and now, an inheritance we have a right to obtain. And if he said this, it is because it is true, independently of whether it means anything to you or me at all.

What attitude do people today have to the peace of Christ? This is an important question, because in referring to Christ's peace one is referring to the only peace that has any reality, the only one that truly merits the name and, in comparison with which, all others are, usually, parodies or cheap imitations.

What is peace? Where do you have to go to look for it? I think that maybe the reason there is no peace in the world is that we are not looking for it in the right place, that we are making a mistake looking for it where it is not to be found—thinking that peace depended on factors outside ourselves. The peace of Christ, the peace he left us, does not seem to be the peace for which men are searching. But if they fail to get that peace (because they aren't looking for it and, probably, don't even know of its existence), what are they left with?

If people really did desire peace, then you can be sure they would make a real effort to find it, maybe by checking, first of all, on what causes war. For, if the causes of war are not tackled, is it possible to prevent war breaking out? So, what really does lie at the root of war?

War, in a certain sense and insofar as it is an evil, is something invented by men, not by God. What I mean is that war is a result of sin. Before Adam sinned, everything was operating perfectly, heading for perfection: there was no pain, no disease; no deception, no treachery; no anger, no violence, no war, no death. The original sin of Adam and Eve found man healthy, balanced, sensible, rational, and generous and turned him into someone blemished, selfish, proud, mean, and cruel; this meant that man was unbalanced; the life of every individual was going to be a fight to the finish between opposing tendencies. That is the paradox of the human condition: even in a single individual you can have heroic deeds alongside abject actions, generosity and meanness, love and hate. Everything, really. And the reason for this is that sin is never strong enough totally to wipe out the reflection of God in men: it can go only so far as to blur it, distort it, weaken it; it can wound man's soul but not destroy it; it can allow hatred to get a foothold, but it cannot eliminate man's capacity to love; it can twist his will, but not to the extent that he cannot turn back and mend his ways. Fine; but even though that is true, in practice what happens is that a person who has a blotch on his character tends to follow his inclinations, and his natural inclination (that is, the tendency of his nature after being wounded by sin) is toward evil.

No. Ever since Adam, man has not been naturally good. I know that the philosophers of the eighteenth-century Enlightenment made the hypocritical "discovery" that society is the cause of evil in man: man is good, it is society that renders him bad. Amazingly this out-of-date notion is being "rediscovered" by part of modern youth—and also by some sociologists, psychologists, and psychiatrists. The ultimate reason why everything—including peace—is not working is structures; the structures of society are defective. Our new teachers preach violence: the old structures must be overthrown and replaced by new structures that will make war impossible; and our new musical poets, like modern-day troubadours, talk about going off to war armed with guitars (what a crazy idea!); and our new "religions" promote conscientious objection, a perfectly sensible way of preventing war, provided that everyone else adopts it as well. We see more and more "symbolic gestures," pacifist demonstrations (not always that pacific), and articles in the papers signed by well-known people (often, has-beens).

All to no avail. As far back as you go, there have always been wars, because as far back as you go there has always been sin. The history of mankind is such a constant succession of wars that lectures on it in college are a total bore—and not only for the student. It is always the same, and, although the direct causes and the actual events differ from case to case, the underlying reasons are all the same. Injustice, ambition, pride, greed, selfishness—this is what unleashes war, this is the charge that explodes as soon as you press the button. And when, at the end of every war, peace is made (though years can go by between the cease fire and the signing), the very treaty itself almost always carries within it the germ of the next war—new rancor, new fears, new revenge.

That is the way the world is, and that is the way it will stay. In this connection, I don't think Jesus had any illusions on the matter: he knew that sin would not go away and, therefore, that its effects, including war, would remain with us. Yet, despite this prospect, he gave peace to his disciples; he left them his peace. Not peace as the world gives or understands it, but something more stable, more reliable; something that is not dependent on the whims or temper of others; something that is not at the mercy of some cabinet minister or of the political party in power or of the greed of men bent on getting even richer; something that is not at the mercy of the fanaticism of those who preach ideology or of those who specialize in organizing revolutions to bring in "a new social order." Something which not even pain, suffering, or opposition can destroy, because none of these things can get within reach of the solid bases on which that peace rests.

The peace of Christ, that peace which he gave his disciples (which he gives to those who believe in him), is the outcome of sanctifying grace. Just as war is the outcome of sin. And you can be sure that not everyone is going to find this peace—although it is there for the finding. No, his peace is only for men of good will, and someone who does not have good will cannot even envisage attaining this peace.

Marxists have proven how clever they are by seeing religion—faith in Christ, and all that it involves—as the greatest obstacle to the utopia. Rid man of God, destroy man's hope of attaining eternal happiness, and what has he left? Only a fight to the death to get as much of the action as he can in this world. Marx knew what he was doing when he spelled out that the way to accelerate the inevitable (as he saw it) course of history was not through peace but through war and violent revolution. After taking God away from us, he left us with violence, and in compensation he asked us to believe firmly in that earthly paradise which inexorably lies ahead.

Nor is our neo-capitalistic society less stupid. It also wants people to be happy, and in the name of human welfare it controls births and, without declaring war on life, legalizes voluntary abortion. And then it self-righteously condemns violence and bemoans the horrors of war.

But they all, Marxists and neo-capitalists alike, talk about peace; they incessantly talk about preserving peace and about working for peace. Tell me: Is that a sign of good will? Is there good will in the world, among men? Just look around, just glance at the papers. Above all, look at yourselves, at your conscience. Do you have peace of soul? No one gives what he does not have, because if he does not have it, how can he give it? Who is going to give peace to the world—a bunch of people who are incapable even of keeping their own souls at peace?

I have the impression that people nowadays do not really desire peace; at most what they want is the absence of conflict. It seems as if they are keener on obtaining external peace—the peace to which Merton was referring—than interior peace—the peace Saint-Exupéry was trying to describe. It also seems as if they are more inclined toward external violence and violence toward others (even if that involves war) than they are to do interior violence to themselves—which is the only route to take to find peace. The only route, because sin, which is the origin of war, violence, and enmity, can be attained only by doing violence to one's ego. Pacifists never attain peace: only peacemakers do. Blessed are the peacemakers, because they will be called children of God (see Mt 5:9)! And our God is a God of peace.

Peace, let me repeat, is not something for everyone; only men of good will can attain it, because it belongs only to those who conquer it by fighting their own selfishness, by fighting those evil tendencies we all carry inside us, which we strive to satisfy, at all costs. And not everyone strives in that kind of way. "I can never have real happiness if I have no peace. And what is peace? Peace is something intimately associated with war. Peace is the result of victory. Peace demands of me a continual struggle. Without that struggle, I'll never be able to have peace." *

What about you: Are you putting up a fight? You know very well that I'm not referring to armed conflict between states or to the sort of fighting that urban guerrillas or revolutionary or antirevolutionary commandos engage in or the less ambitious kind of struggle that takes the form of painting slogans and symbols on walls and signboards to show your protest or enthusiasm and, incidentally, to annoy your neighbor. I'm referring to

*St. Josemaría Escrivá de Balaguer, *The Way*, no. 308.

something much more difficult—the cutting off of the heads of the monstrous hydra of sensuality and impurity (although, I suppose, believers in Freud may see this as repression), lies and hypocrisy (first our own and if, before we die, we obtain good results, then perhaps we might think of doing something about other people's lies and hypocrisy), covetousness and caprice, and pride over petty little things; backbiting, easygoingness, and all the other defects we might list.

As I see it, it is all a matter of having good will. And we are getting nowhere because we do not have that good will. If we are not ready to stop making war on God by committing sins, there is no good will around. And if we do not have good will toward God, who has given us life, who became man and died in order to redeem us from sin and death, and did all that simply because he loves us (Saint John says, "He loved us" [1 Jn 4: 10]—have you ever thought about that?); if we do not have good will toward God, how and in the name of what can we have good will toward others?

When a person does not have good will toward God, he does not have peace. A man who lets sin enter his soul has opened the door to hatred and has made himself a slave of the devil. (Yes, the devil exists, the devil is real.) Deep down, his soul is in turmoil. This man is at war with God and with himself, and it is not at all easy for him to promote peace in the world, or even to promote peace among those around him. To think that you can deal with a disease by alleviating its symptoms and doing nothing about its causes is stupid and laughable. To think that making speeches about peace and singing protest songs about war is going to change the world because it is going to change men—that is, I think, to be naïve. In fact, it amazes me how people, apparently as clever as they think themselves to be, can really think like that, can use their intelligence to deceive themselves as easily as that.

The peace of Christ, the peace he gave us, does not, it seems, very much attract contemporary men, not even those who call themselves Catholics; a world that crucified Jesus Christ also rejects his peace: it is a kind of peace that doesn't interest them because it means they have to stir themselves, deprive themselves of things (but only of harmful things, though they may appear to be good), and keep up a continuous struggle; and man today (I mean, man in the consumer society: competition, standards of living, night clubs, computers, air pollution, moral pollution, the UN, UNESCO, and so on) is taken up with so many highly important matters that he has no time, no tranquility, no desire, to stop to check whether all this about the peace of Christ is anything more than a phrase the Pope brings up every now and then in an address.

So, you see how things are: I want you to have peace. For you are young people, and happiness is (sorry, it should be) your inheritance, and happiness is not possible without interior peace. I have seen many of you laugh . . . but some people, I notice, laugh only with their mouths, not with their eyes. In some eyes I have seen sadness, as if they were already defeated; in others, restlessness, as if they felt uncomfortable; or hardness and resentment, as if the world owed them something they were going to make sure they got, one way or another; and other eyes, forgive me, I saw to be unclean, dirty, with the light extinguished. And in others I don't know what there was, because they never looked me straight in the face.

Don't deceive yourselves, don't try to deceive yourselves, like those little children who cover their eyes and face the wall and say, "I'm not here." The peace of the dead, the peace of those who are under an anesthetic, the peace of those who are "blissfully" unaware (that is, of those who have no conscience), the peace of those who have been brutalized: that is not peace. None of that brings man happiness—true happiness, not its artificial substitute.

Nowadays young people are all in favor of peace, and although, in general, they say they are pacifists, I would not dare to say that they are peacemakers; at least some of them are not. To be peacemakers, to create peace all around oneself, to make the scene pleasant and calm, our own inner lives need to be tranquil and allow something of the love God has for us to find a place in our soul. And this, for someone who is not constantly fighting against sin (despite what all the modern experts say), is as impossible as defeating a well-equipped army with songs and guitars. Suppress sin in the world, and you will have suppressed war. Yet, even in a world that is in sin and at war, the peace of Christ is possible for everyone.

4

Repentance

"You will all likewise perish."

"You will all likewise perish" (Lk 13:5). When we read these words or hear them quoted on their own, our immediate reaction is one of irritation. They instinctively repel us. They have a threatening tone about them; they ring of intolerance, negativity, rigorism; we don't even want to explore what they mean; we want to shut them out. They remind us of times gone by, when we had to fend off ideas like condemnation, hell, the terrible judgment following on death, fear of eternity—all those things people tend to think no longer apply but which, nevertheless, are absolutely certain and real even if we don't want to hear of them, even if we reject them as affronts to human dignity.

Yet these words, which we are going to think about now, were spoken by Jesus Christ, and they are there in the Gospel for everyone to read. Of course, they are not as roughly presented as I have given them. It is dangerous to take a phrase out of context; that usually makes for misunderstanding; we can get not only its tone wrong, but its meaning as well.

The words in question come from a passage in Saint Luke (13:1–5) and form a part of some teaching Jesus gave his disciples in connection with a recent event they had been telling him about.

> There were some present at that very time who told him of the Galileans whose blood Pilate had mingled with their sacrifices. And he answered them, "Do you think

43

that these Galileans were worse sinners than all the other Galileans, because they suffered thus? I tell you, No; but unless you repent you will all likewise perish. Or those eighteen upon whom the tower in Siloam fell and killed them, do you think that they were worse offenders than all the others who dwelt in Jerusalem? I tell you, No; but unless you repent you will all likewise perish."

So you can see that Jesus did say these words, but the context in which he said them takes away the roughness, the tone of ill humor and coldness, that you get if you hear them on their own. He was simply drawing their attention to something that would certainly happen, if they did not take steps to prevent it from happening.

Even so, these words do not constitute a consoling piece of doctrine. They are not reassuring and joyful, like the parable of the prodigal son or the story of Mary Magdalen, for example. Rather, they belong to that other kind of teaching where Jesus tried hard to show us that salvation, getting to heaven, is not an easy matter: a person needs to work hard to achieve salvation; it calls for more than good will or an occasional good action done in the course of one's lifetime. It is not as if we were Boy Scouts, who do their good deed every day and can go to bed happy that they have done what is required of them. It is something much more serious than that.

"Unless you repent, unless you do penance, you will all likewise perish." Does this mean that penance is *necessary* for salvation, necessary to avoid perishing for all eternity? I can't see what else it can mean. Obviously, Jesus was not referring to physical death: everyone, whether he does penance or not, has to die, one way or another. But if the words refer to eternal death, then we must conclude that there is no salvation without penance.

It would not surprise me if you found this conclusion annoying on the grounds that it means you have to comply with a condition as unnecessary as it is capricious, as annoying as it is arbitrary. But anyone who reacts in this way should dismiss this reaction. This ignorance of basic truths shows that he is the victim of consumer society propaganda, well on the way to losing his faith, a faith whose content is fading from his mind.

That's the way it is: the words of the Gospel do sound strange to those who are described as "the people of our time." The idea of penance does not make sense when the faith is twisted to suit the consumer. Penance implies some connection with sin, with an offense against God that needs to be atoned for. But how can you have atonement when you deny that any offense has been committed? When God is understood in a vague deistic sort of way or when the notion of personal sin is replaced by the notion of social sins, which dilute responsibility to the point of doing away with it, what kind of meaning can sin have? Sin becomes an empty meaningless word.

The first step a person must take if he is to realize that penance does make sense is to recognize that he is a sinner. Everyone is a sinner; that is to say, he is in debt to God. I don't say this lightly—look what Saint John says: "If we say we have no sin, we deceive ourselves, and the truth is not in us. If we confess our sins, he is faithful and just, and will forgive our sins and cleanse us from all unrighteousness. If we say we have not sinned, we make him a liar, and his word is not in us" (1 Jn 1:8–10). This means that penance becomes a matter of justice: a debtor is under an obligation to pay what he owes. Here we meet the first difficulty toward understanding that penance is necessary, for people's general attitude these days—more influenced by human theories than by the truths of revelation—is not inclined to see man as a debtor who must pay up.

The root of penance lies in repentance, contrition,

being grieved at the harm we have done an innocent person, at the wound we have opened by offending someone who has a right to our respect, friendship, and love. This grief (*me poenitet* is the Latin expression: I am weighed down) is what leads us to recognize our fault, to seek forgiveness, and, indeed, to place ourselves at the disposition of the offended party and do what we can to repair the harm we have done. When sorrow is sincere, the sinner feels a genuine need to demonstrate with deeds that he really wants to wipe out his wrongdoing. He really wants to atone to the person he has offended. This is why, in the real situation, acts of penance have a direct connection with our sense of sorrow for sin committed.

So: what is sin? I am afraid that really it is not a subject that greatly interests people nowadays unless it is approached in a modern way, in keeping with the degree of "maturity" mankind has achieved. There are all sorts of "modern" approaches to sin. For example, mature modern man is not only interested in but very open to theories that suggest that sin is simply a guilt complex, which can easily be cured by an expert psychoanalyst; he also likes theories that say that sin is just a taboo, from which you have to free yourself because it cramps your personality and traps you in a thicket of bourgeois conventionalism; or theories that state that sin is an unimportant accident, the result of psychological causes—not something to worry about, because no one can be blamed for sinning. Perhaps the theory people like most is that which sees sin only in terms of "social sin," community sin: this exonerates the individual from all personal responsibility without having to go as far as deny the very existence of sin.

These theories to which I have referred are actually doing the rounds and making inroads in the minds of many Christians, which shows that we have done very little to take issue with the false teaching spread by pseudotheologians and pseudoscientists (God alone knows why they have developed these theories); nor have we done much about making sure we, for our part, have a good grasp of Christian doctrine.

However, I must remind you that sin is, essentially and above all, an offense against God. It is man rebelling against his Creator, rupturing his link with God. It amounts to despising Christ's sufferings and the reason he underwent them. Compared with all that, other dimensions of sin do not amount to much—not even the harm sin does our neighbor—because that arises out of the fact that our neighbor is one of God's creatures, made in his image and likeness; it is God whom we are hurting when we hurt our neighbor (if we can put it that way). Without God, who created him and keeps him in existence, there would be no neighbor, no man, no universe. There would be nothing.

Through Adam's enormous sin, mankind rejected God; and by the time people realized the catastrophe they had drawn down on themselves it was too late. But God is our Father, a Father whose love for his children ("God is love," 1 Jn 4:8) led him to have his only-begotten Son take on human nature in the womb of the Virgin Mary and die nailed to a Cross to atone for our sins (for all sins, from Adam's to the last sin of the last man on earth), in payment of a debt that no man, nor mankind as a whole, had any way of paying. Christ's sacrifice paid the entire sum of that debt.

But does man, every man, accept this ransom paid on his behalf? It can happen that he refuses to accept that he has any debt to pay—in which case he voluntarily excludes himself from redemption. This seems to be the attitude of those who say there is no such thing as sin or

who make sin out to be something so banal and insig-
nificant that redemption (the crucifixion of the Son of
God!) becomes meaningless, and any act of atonement
something silly and useless. Whereas man's recognition
that he is a sinner, his acceptance of Christ's payment of
his debt, expresses itself in a gesture of good will—
penance.

We live in a very easygoing time. True, there is a lot
of harshness and violence, but it is harshness and violence done to others, the cruelty typical of the weak.
Nowhere can we find that violence which everyone
should do to himself, to keep his instincts under control,
to dominate his will and make it serve God, make it do
what it ought to do, regardless of whether or not that is
comfortable or pleasant. The softness typical of our society expresses itself in the way we coddle our body, in our
apparently insatiable search for well being; in flight from
all forms of discomfort; in our frantic pursuit of pleasure,
of everything that indulges our senses. This elaborate
orchestration to do with sex, from childhood onward
(children must be given sexual education as early as
possible), the whole industry in favor of a better standard of living, comfort, plenty (including plenty of
contraceptives): all this is geared to making man forget
that life is really nothing more than "a bad night in a bad
inn," as Saint Teresa put it.

Today, the classical forms of penance (fasting, hair
shirts, the discipline, vigils) which used to be so much in
favor, seem to most Christians to be senseless. Very little
seems to be said about doing penance for one's sins; the
emphasis, rather, is on improving living standards to
give people access to a more dignified and more comfortable kind of life. The kind of person created by the mature world of today (a world that "sins insolently and
abhors atonement for sin," as Pope Paul VI put it) is

capable of making huge sacrifices in the name of science, technology, power, wealth, and even sport; but what about God, who was crucified for our sins? "What great fear people have of atonement! If what they do to please the world were done with a purified intention for God, what saints many would be!" (*The Way*, no. 215).

It is so true. Many people do, for no reason at all, what, if done in a spirit of expiation, could bring peace to their souls and maybe make saints of them. "Hippies," for example, let their hair grow. The Nazarites of olden times also refrained from cutting their hair to show that they were dedicated to God, but for people today it is simply a form of protest. Many young people go around looking filthy—just like any repentant medieval noble making up to God for his years of slavery to worldly pleasure by going around in rags. But nowadays people are doing it just because they "let things go," in the name of freedom. If someone, voluntarily and out of love for Christ crucified, imposed on himself the penance of going out in the early morning on a cold, miserable day to climb a mountain in the wind and the rain, people would probably laugh at him or think him mad. But they think it quite in order for someone to go out on a hunt in the same conditions. People today can see no point in striving to keep their instinct under control, but if a woman starves herself to keep in shape or a man past forty trains to keep fit, that meets with their entire approval. A desire to keep trim or the fear of getting a heart attack have more influence on a Christian today than eagerness to get to heaven or fear of hell. Just look at the training astronauts undergo. Read the books they have written: the fathers of the desert were schoolboys compared with them. Take that young Prague student who set fire to himself to protest against the 1968 Soviet invasion of his country; everyone applauded him. People seem ready to accept someone committing suicide to protest against injustice, but they cannot see any sense in a man doing penance for his sins. If Christians took a leaf out of the book of the athlete who goes to enormous pains to knock a second off his record (what does it matter, really?) and did as much to atone to God for the sins they have committed, I think there would be a lot more sanctity in the world.

No: man in the technological era simply does not admit that he has anything for which to atone, any debt to repay to God. And yet . . .

If you have read Georges Bernanos, you may have been surprised by the terrible sense of sin that exists in the society, in the people who make up the society, that he describes. He so accurately conveys the sinister atmosphere of sin in the environment that you can almost smell it; it stains everything; it seems to contaminate even the air people breathe. Bernanos was writing at a time when external appearances were given great importance (a hypocritical society) and righteous people were all very conscious of their respectability; convention was their god. We don't find that sort of thing nowadays; there are no righteous around. Today all conventions have been torn down, and we don't hide our vices under a cloak of respectability (we are so open and honest!). No. We have decided that vice is respectable, and there is no reason to hide it. It is not a sin; it is something natural (even vices that are against nature); so, instead of hiding our vices, we parade them, which means that we are more hypocritical than the righteous people of a hypocritical society. They lied to other people by hiding their sins, but they did not lie to themselves or think that other people were half-wits; in other words, they lived in a real world; they called a spade a spade. Today, the people of our mature society lie to themselves and to other people as well. The righteous of a previous era were whitened sepulchers, but they did not succeed in deceiving anyone because, whitened though they were, they did not hide the fact that they were sepulchers. Today's sepulchers are whitened, but they pretend they are not tombs but living monuments erected in the name of freedom and progress, and as such they demand to be accepted. And they think that other people are fools and do not see through them. And sometimes they are quite right.

Today's Pharisees do not admit sin; they will not accept that they are sinners. They have nothing in common with the publican in the Gospel, who was such a sinner that he did not even dare enter the Temple. He stayed at the entrance, half hidden by a pillar, in case anyone should think he was profaning the Temple by his presence, and not daring to raise his head. He stayed there, head bent, beating his breast, saying over and over again, "God, be merciful to me a sinner!" (Lk 18: 13).

Not so the Pharisee. He stood up for all to see, his head high (the dignity of man!), pleased with himself, giving thanks that he was not a sinner. He paid his tithes, he was not an adulterer, or a thief—not like that despicable publican. Today's Pharisee is not a sinner either, because what he does is not sin: he has none of those guilt complexes, he has shed them all; he has freed himself of conventions and taboos, and even of any trace of objective moral standards. He is liberated. But we should not make him the equal of the Pharisee in the Gospel, even though he too holds his head high. The Pharisee in the Gospel still gave thanks to God.

As Saint Teresa used say, when she wandered off and lost the thread of what she was writing, "I've got side-tracked once again!" What I meant to say was that sin is a fact: it is the worst, the most abominable of all facts; it is pure evil, but it is absolutely real. And, second, you and I and everyone are sinners: we are people born in sin and forever in God's debt; people who, of our own accord, have offended God through personal sins; people, therefore, who have no right to look at God with our heads held high, because our "human dignity" (which comes from our being the image and likeness of God, and from being redeemed by the blood of Christ) is something we have trampled on by behaving in a way that is beneath the dignity of man.

Are you conscious of this? The Church certainly is. The Church knows that she is the mystical Body of Christ and that we are members of that Body. If Christ, the Head, suffered on account of our sins, it is only right that we, members of his Body, should be in solidarity with him—if the innocent paid for the guilty, surely the guilty have to do something themselves.

The Church, I repeat, has always known that penance was necessary for salvation. And because she knows her own responsibility and is well aware of our softness, she laid down that we should all do a minimum of penance, in the form of fasting and abstinence. Not a great deal, just a minimum. This law was in force for centuries. Now she has decided to leave it to the generosity of the faithful and to their love of God to decide what acts of penance to do, leaving us free to substitute other good deeds for fasting and abstinence. She has put the ball into our court, taken away the crutches we were using. This new situation, where the burden of doing penance lies squarely on our shoulders, can help us see whether what we did in the past was because of our desire to make reparation for our sins, our sorrow for having offended God, our compassion for Christ crucified on our behalf, or simply the residue of a long-established custom that we found trite and, at times, even meaningless. Now we can indeed know whether as Catholics we are adults or still children.

I don't want to scandalize you, yet I cannot treat you like people who cannot be told the hard truth. The mystery of iniquity, sin, is something very real and very serious. So much so that, if one single sin could prevent a war (with all the suffering that means for innocent parties), if one single sin could wipe out hunger and thirst, pain, and physical death, it still would not be licit to commit it. Sin is worse than all the evils it gives rise to. And hunger and thirst and pains, war and death and suffering, are just some of the results of the first sin man committed—results multiplied over and over again by all the sins that followed it. And today people seem to be bent on multiplying them, to judge from how eager some are to convince us that sin is a mere trifle—yet a highly pleasant and necessary course to take to attain "personal fulfillment."

There is a great mystery in this terrible impoverishment that sin creates wherever it is to be found, and the world today has become a huge bed of worms. Somewhere, there must be saints who love God and are consumed with sorrow at the affronts Christ is bearing with infinite patience—otherwise the world would just collapse. And there is also a culpable emptyheadedness (or should we say ignorance?) in the banal and unconcerned attitude we adopt toward sin. For very many Catholics sin is just an accident, which seems to have very little impact on their lives. There are people who habitually go around dead on the inside, in a state of condemnation and in the power of the devil, and who do nothing to change. Perhaps because they are, simply, dead.

I don't want to deceive you, which is what some people seem intent on doing. If we do not do penance, if we do not really repent and turn to God, we will all likewise perish. Penance is not a luxury; it is a necessity (presuming, of course, that we want to live eternally with Christ. If that is not what we want, if we want something else, then obviously we should do other things than penance.) I do realize that this whole business of penance is not very pleasant, but it's not meant to be. Not even Jesus tried to win us over by smiles, concessions, and condescension. He spoke by his actions; he told us truths, whether pleasant or not. What he did not do was buy us by flattery—by useless, stupid lies. No, he did what none of those false prophets do who swarm all over the place preaching that what God forbids is good and that what he commands is bad for us: he gave his life to pay our debts.

And if it is true that you young people have an instinct for justice, if it is true that you have a great sensitivity for detecting injustice wherever it lies hidden, how is it that you tolerate sin, which is the greatest injustice of all, given that it is an affront and an offense to God, to whom we owe our very existence? Why are you so tolerant; why do you cooperate in condemning Jesus Christ as if he were an imposter?

"Unless you repent you will all likewise perish"—I think it is all very just. A person cannot go through life hating God and crucifying his Son and, on top of that, think that he is being unjustly treated because he is not given eternal life on a plate. You cannot be intellectually indifferent to Christ's Passion or actively despise it and then claim that that very Passion is your passport to heaven. You just cannot.

5

The Church's Language

"Why do you not understand what I say?"

To judge by this question, which Jesus asked in the course of one of those exchanges with the Pharisees that occurred every so often, it would seem that the world today has nothing to teach the Pharisees about "communication breakdown."

The whole subject of communication breakdown is very much in vogue. Young people—especially young "intellectuals"—use this tag to indicate that they don't understand their parents, nor do their parents understand them; that there exists a huge generation gap: the old and the young do not communicate. The same sort of problem also exists between the Church and the world today, if we are to go by what religious affairs commentators have to say (they seem to be rather a noisy bunch, though it may be merely artificial noise created by the news media).

I'd like to look a little closer at this latter kind of communication breakdown. I would not be surprised if it were one of the main contributors to the confusion of ideas on religious matters that is typical of young people today . . . and typical of adults as well. I know that this confusion is not something you have caused yourselves, but, I think, something that has been passed on to you by your teachers, who, in their turn, have observed it and tenaciously held on to it.

I dare say that many people within the Church are proposing ways and means to repair this breakdown in communication between the Church and the world. Naturally; they feel full of good will toward that paganized world which has turned its back on God and yet is going from strength to strength as far as science and technology are concerned; they really feel for these people whose only intelligible language is that of mature, modern man. Certainly the world has come a long way since the time of the Council of Trent. Advances in science and technology, new philosophies, radical changes in people's outlook, whole new ways of life. The Church—people are saying—should take note of this evolution and evolve along with it. They talk about Christian thinking being inadequate in the present situation; the Church, they say, uses "archaic language" in preaching the message of salvation. The Church, they argue—the Church as a whole and each of its members—needs to make her own the outlook pressed upon her by modern society.

Although the content of this sort of religious writing is all very much the same, the tone used varies considerably. At times, a certain bitterness is in evidence—in accusing the Church of getting it all wrong for ages and saying that the time has come for her to shake herself and get up to date so as to make herself understood.

At other times the tone is somewhat pained: the writer has thought things out, but it is as if he were giving advice with infinite patience because the Church is old and a bit backward and finds it very difficult to change her attitude. Other writings are breezy, enthusiastic, and triumphalistic—typical of religious-affairs correspondents when they cover the "revival" of the Church and the great pioneering work being done by the "with-it" theologians and pastors who somehow or other have managed to cut through a whole jungle of dead wood and have begun to put the Church in touch with the world once more.

Well, I'm not going to say that there is no basis at all for this sort of criticism, but, if I'm to be sincere, I must add that we should not blame the Church for the short-comings of her members, even if they be ecclesiastics. In fact, the confusion arises out of the unfortunate use of a language we might term "ecclesiastical" or, not to put too fine a point on it, "clerical"—a language not spoken by the ordinary man in the street. And not merely the language but also its tone, its formulas, its styles, and even the thought structures behind it. However, all these things were not really things for which the Church could be held responsible. They were created by various ecclesiastics and by lay people who, for one reason or another, were pulled into this kind of "clericalized world"—all of whom were quite out of touch with the rest of the world. People at large, maybe, got the idea that "that" was Catholicism or that to be a true-blue Catholic you really had to be like that and speak that peculiar language; and, if the truth be known, they didn't like that scene and they just did not feel up to making the effort to get into it.

Well, I doubt very much if this is what these critics are trying to put right. And also I have my doubts about whether the new language that they are using and pro-posing we use is the right one for converting the world to God—for all kinds of reasons, one being that this new language is not in fact any clearer; it is more obscure. They say (and I quote) that "along with the news the doctrine of kerygma is also being proposed," and al-though this indeed must be consoling for the Christian faithful, I cannot see most of them understanding what it means.

They say that between God, who wants to talk to man, and man, who is quite ready to listen to God, communication just isn't happening because there is a screen in the way and that screen is "a language that is completely outside modern man's experience." But I am afraid they give a very restrictive meaning to the expression "modern man," or a very ambiguous one. One gets the impression that when they refer to man today they mean the scientist or the technologist or the philosopher—but never the man in the street. And it still remains to be seen whether "modern man" is, in fact, inclined to listen to God. Besides, what is all this about language having to fit in with man's "experience"? What do they mean when they say they are all in favor of formulating or "expressing" the teaching of the Gospel in a way suited to the mentality of modern man?

I don't think they mean anything like what I am going to tell you now, which is something I read in a book that appeared not so long ago. At least, I hope not. The author called on "the Christians of our time to interrogate the Gospel for its relevance to political thought and activity." The real aim of Christianity, he argued, was to get "people to make their way forward in dialogue." And, asking why it was that Christ chose not to "entangle himself" in temporal matters (matters, however, which people are so terribly keen to get the Church to take a stand on nowadays), he threw out these leading questions: "Was he trying to keep his hands clean? Did he not realize the importance of politics? Did he have a 'disincarnated' notion of religion?"

I ask you: Do you think that you can put questions like that to the Word of God, who became man in the womb of the Virgin Mary in order to reveal to us the mystery of God, one and three? Do you think that that is the way to set about expressing the good news in appropriate language? Really, that sort of "theological" writing would make you laugh, were it not so sad. In fact, it really makes you cry, because you are pained by the blindness of the writers in question or by the confusion they are sowing in the minds of Christians or on both scores.

Is it really the case that the Gospel message is unintelligible to the world today because the Church insists on continuing to express it in terms, concepts, and experience that belong to a world that is dead and gone? Let's look a little deeper into this.

Language is made up of words, and a word, by definition, expresses an idea. It is useful to bear in mind, at the very outset, that, if this is the case, then, if you change a word, you are changing an idea. Whether you stayed true to revelation or became an Arian heretic, all hinged on two words: "consubstantial with" or "similar to"; that was the difference. But in Greek the two words were almost identical. The Church, which holds the deposit of revelation, has always had a great respect for words, choosing them very carefully to make sure they express the content of revelation as precisely and accurately as possible.

It is true that on the level of human affairs such basic ideas as there are are expressed by philosophy. However, revelation has to do essentially with God and the supernatural world, which, as you can understand, is quite beyond the natural capacity of human reason. If, out of all the philosophies there are and all the languages available, you have to choose one to express, in a way accessible to the human mind and as faithfully and as exactly as possible, the message of salvation, then someone must decide which language and which philosophy to use, which terms are best suited to the task.

And who is equipped to decide which philosophy, out of all the philosophies available, best expresses in human terms, in human concepts, the supernatural truths that God has revealed? Undoubtedly, the Church. The deposit of revelation has been entrusted to the Church, not just to protect it but to teach it to men until the end of time, for as long as there are men on earth. The Church, and only the Church, has been given the authority to interpret the meaning of Scripture correctly and infallibly. It is therefore for the Church to decide which philosophy, which language, is best suited to explaining revealed truths, divine mysteries, to the extent that it is possible to make them intelligible to the human mind.

It took centuries for this to happen, but this is not the place to examine the process. The fact is that the Church has made its choice and, until it finds a better medium, the medium it has chosen is what is called "the philosophy of being," Aristotelian-Thomistic philosophy. Up to now and in the judgment of the Church (and if there is anyone who can make that judgment it is the Church) that philosophy is the one best suited to express the message of revelation in human terms.

But, apparently, nowadays, there are people who do not see eye to eye with this decision. They say that these now traditional philosophical terms have not kept pace with scientific discoveries and just do not fit the mentality of people today; and they are putting the pressure on for a change of language, a change of philosophy. In other words, a change of ideas.

There is nothing new about all this. When I was reading Saint Augustine's treatises on the Gospel of Saint John, there was a phrase that caught my attention: justifying his giving emphasis to a particular passage, Augustine said, "Let no one, let no weigher of words, no examiner of syllables, on the grounds that he knows Latin, start correcting the word of God." Have no fear: I'm not going to give you a detailed historical rundown: I will refer only to the attempts made by modernism, toward the end of the nineteenth century, to relativize dogma by introducing certain changes in its wording (always in line with the philosophy currently in fashion), attempts that were frustrated at the time by the vigilance and energy of Pope Saint Pius X, not a very popular figure in certain circles these days.

It wasn't the language that they wanted to change at that time; nor was it a change of language that a group of "theologians" were calling for thirty years ago when they proclaimed the need for a new theology, suited to the modern world. All this talk about "nature" and "person," "matter" and "form," "substance" and "accident," "cause" and "effect" (they were saying), all these concepts used in speaking of the Trinity, the Incarnation, the Eucharist—they are archaic, completely outmoded. If you want to get the world to accept dogmas, they went on, then you have to change the wording, and express the dogmas in contemporary philosophical concepts, because every age has its own language, its own outlook, so you cannot get revealed truths across if you express them in archaic language that is beyond their experience. These new "theologians," and their successors at the present time, say that "if we want Christ to retain the qualities on which his authority and our adoration are based, the best approach, not to say the only approach, is to go right along with the most up-to-date ideas about evolution." Body and soul, matter and spirit: these are just stages in cosmic evolution toward the Omega Point. Angels? Absurd! Angel is just a name for a point in the evolutionary process. Original sin? A way of describing a primitive stage of mankind. Grace? One stage more in evolution, a little ahead of nature, but not essentially distinct from it. And so on and so on. Obviously, given that sort of approach, there is an urgent need to demythologize, to desacralize. And so they tell us that the "Incarnation is not really the Word taking on human nature"; what it means is "the presence of the Christian among men": away with myths, which the mature world rejects (it is mature enough for that), and let's find a way of saying something that people will find acceptable!

No. What is in question is not a simple change of wording, but a change in the content of revelation, a watering-down of Christ's teaching. Every now and again this sort of thing happens. If you read the Fathers of the Church you will see how they thunder against falsifications of doctrine, which, by one method or another, people were propagating with a zeal worthy of a better cause.

The interesting thing is—and maybe this explains the spread of the present confusion—that way-out ideas of this kind have taken root in certain sectors where you would have expected people to accept fully the teaching of Jesus Christ, an acceptance whose firmness would be matched by the denunciation of false teaching and clear explanation of the deposit of faith. But that is another matter, which we won't go into now.

What Jesus said to the Pharisees was: "Why do you not understand what I say? It is because you cannot bear to hear my word" (Jn 8:43). He was so right. Accepting Christ's teaching and putting it into practice meant changing their whole direction. They had mutilated revelation where possible and bent it to suit their own convenience by distorting its meaning where mutilation would not work because it would have been so barefaced that they would have lost whatever ground they did have to get the people to follow them. What the Pharisees wanted was a form of revelation that would confirm their own tastes and earthly aspirations, but they could not stand any teaching that would mean renouncing their own ideas. The only language they wanted to hear was their own, even if their own salvation was at stake.

Exactly the same thing is happening at present, and with the same hypocrisy. Where it is not possible to mutilate revelation language to adapt it to the "categories" of man today, to his "experience," by this simple method they falsify revelation and destroy it. Like the Jews of Jesus' time they say, "This is a hard saying; who can listen to it?" Certainly not people whose pride will not admit any law other than that made by themselves. Neither can dirt bear cleanliness, nor is chastity acceptable to a man who lives for sex; people who adore money are not interested in poverty; and a supernatural transcendental revelation is intolerable to a world that wants to concern itself only with what it has itself created or can itself control.

This kind of thinking has had a great impact, among other reasons, because of the tremendous power of the media, the skill of its proponents, the passivity of people who ought to have spoken out at certain times, and also, perhaps, because of the collaboration given by Christians who are not well-instructed in their faith or who are too caught up by the spirit of this world.

Every science has its own terminology. If there are not words to describe new methods, new phenomena or discoveries, they are invented. No one asks physics or biology to change its terminology to make it easier for the ordinary man to understand; on the contrary, it is up to the layman to have an open attitude if he wants to understand scientific truths: he has to learn whatever terminology is necessary. And when a person with a vocation to be a teacher really *knows* a science, he can always find the right language to put it across to others. For centuries the Church spoke a language accessible to scholars and to ordinary people, even to children. The Christian faithful have always known, through the old language (well tested by time) what was essential in the mysteries of faith. Yes, one does need to be very open to learning about something when one knows nothing about it. People largely understood the teaching, which Jesus gave them in a manner suited to their mentality, and what they did not understand they took on faith. Some of the Pharisees did indeed understand it, and they eventually became disciples of our Lord. Only those who were not ready to put his teaching into practice failed to understand his language, but their attitude was a hypocritical attitude, as Jesus pointed out. The fault did not lie in the language, but in their interior obstinacy in not listening to any language other than the one they wanted to hear.

So you can see how "communication breakdown," one of the great catch phrases of our time, can be just another of those artificially blown-up balloons, which, if someone manages to pinch it one of these days, will change into a limp, crinkled bit of rubber, with no content at all, no glamour left. I do recognize that communication between someone who speaks and someone who stops his ears because he does not want to listen to what is being said to him, for no other reason (though it may be reason enough) than that he doesn't like it, is impossible. But it is not the language that is to blame.

I don't think that Hegel is any clearer or more intelligible to modern man than Saint Thomas, or that Heidegger uses vocabulary or concepts that are any better than Aristotle's. Far less do I believe that Marx's *Das Kapital* is any easier for the man in the street than Saint Teresa's *Foundations*. Yet I don't hear anyone asking Marx to speak a new language. But you don't have to take my word for it; nor do I ask you to. Just go and read a few pages of Heidegger and a few pages of Saint Thomas, and you can draw your own conclusions.

Personally, I don't think that all this complication of

the language and "expression" of the Gospel message—
or, better still, "inferiority complex" about language—
that all this talk, which is more intellectual than pastoral
and more theoretical than practical, conveys even a mod-
erate idea of Jesus Christ, of the Gospel, and of the
rudiments of Catholic doctrine. The truths we have to
believe, the commandments of God we ought to keep, the
worship we should render, the sacraments we should
receive—all these do not change. I say it again, what the
Church has to try to do is to get across to people the
ideas that most faithfully express God's revelation to
men. If the world today does not like the language used
and prefers other ideas, then that's its affair. The Pharisees didn't like Jesus' language either, but Jesus did not
change it and say what they wanted to hear. I get the
impression that what the world today—and the "theologians" who have appointed themselves as spokesmen of
its aspirations—is asking is this: a kind of brainwashing,
whereby the Church will shed her supernatural preten-
sions, abdicate her divine origin, and accommodate revelation to the ideologies that happen to be in fashion.

I do recognize the good will of simple people who do
everything possible to try to adapt language—in this
case, words—to modern times. It is quite moving to see
liturgists, when translating the texts of Holy Scripture
into the vernacular, sensitively jettisoning the word "servant" for "employee," on the grounds that it is more
suited to the mentality of man today. It is quite moving,
but I don't believe that pastoral methods of this sort
attract many sheep into the fold.

Audio-visual language is also being changed—a language that can contribute much to the education of ordinary people. The organ is giving way to electric guitars,
Gregorian chant to pop and rock: perhaps this is a
shedding of out-of-date styles in favor of what is called

modern culture. The spokesmen of the "world of today" have no liking, either, for a language of sculpture that depicts Christ as a man nailed to the Cross, covered in blood, his agony reflected in his eyes, under the crown of thorns, or as wearing a serene, priestly look as he reigns from the Cross; it seems that the world today has no need for realism of that kind, better suited to less adult times, which regarded the sacrifice of Calvary as an event that really happened, something in its own right, not a mere symbol. They think the symbol is better conveyed by those metal crucifixes, stylized and almost invisible, or crosses made of odd bits of scrap metal that evoke the world of work, which shapes man, as Marx says. We see no more—or they are in the process of disappearing—tabernacles that were in the form of a house, in which the Blessed Sacrament lived, Christ himself, body, blood, soul, and divinity; gilded tabernacles decorated with a cross in front; sometimes very rich tabernacles; others made of wood and covered with a white veil as a sign of respect for the immense mystery of the Eucharist. Modest little rectangular boxes, with no cross and no veil, discreetly positioned to one side of the altar or on a side altar or suspended in some way are an expression of the new language of the liturgy, which perhaps is trying to suggest some particular symbolic idea, at the center of which, maybe, lies the notion not of "transubstantiation" but "transignification." It is all a matter of meaning, not of substance, as you can see.

As an explanation (so far as it can be explained) of the mystery of the Incarnation of the Son of God, we used to be told that there are in Jesus Christ two natures (divine and human) and one Person (divine). If a child knew that he knew the basics; I don't mean that he understood it (who can understand a mystery?) but, given the capacity of his mind, knowing that was enough. I would be very interested to know what concepts, what language, can get this truth across to a child in any clearer way.

You may argue that we're not talking about children but about a world that has grown up. Yes, but not grown up as regards revelation, because in that respect the world today is just like the world of the Gentiles in the second century, to take one example, only much more conceited.

More than once—in fact, almost every time I read about "communication breakdown"—I have been puzzled about how it is possible for this problem to exist at a time when the media of communication can reach out everywhere. Nowadays, everything is communicated, and everything is made to be seen, as if privacy didn't exist anymore. I don't know what Samuel Beckett was trying to say in *Waiting for Godot*, but I would have been grateful if he had expressed himself more clearly—assuming that he is trying to express something at all. I don't know which of the many theories put forward to explain the play I should keep. But, of course, this is not the case with the Church. The Church should teach Christ's doctrine clearly, accurately, and exactly; she should not propose clever riddles for intellectual games.

I find this all very trying—and I expect you do too. I just want to conclude with a couple of points that you may find useful, although I think this depends on how concerned you as an individual are to solve, in an honest and serious way, something that affects you directly, something serious. Let's accept that you don't understand the language the Church uses to talk of the mysteries of faith: Are you quite sure that you have made a genuine effort to understand it? Have you, for your part, done that necessary minimum which you do in order to understand what is told you in lectures on physics, biochemistry, or mathematical logic? I'm thinking now of those who very easily stop going to Mass on Sunday because it says nothing to them or because they do not understand why they should go, and of those who don't go to confession because they do not see why this thing or that is a sin.

Or, to put it another way, and going back to the words of the Gospel, given that it apparently is necessary to be ready to practice Jesus' teaching if you really want to understand his language: Are you ready to practice it? Because, if the answer is no, then no one, not even yourselves, can be surprised if you don't understand a word of it.

6

The Church's Role Is Spiritual

"Judge among men."

I would like to begin by commenting on a passage from the Gospel of Saint Luke that relates an episode in Jesus' preaching because I believe it can help clarify some points that, whether we like it or not, are currently being talked about. Saint Luke tells us:

> One of the multitude said to him, "Teacher, bid my brother divide the inheritance with me." But he said to him: "Man, who made me a judge or divider over you?" And he said to them: "Take heed and beware of all covetousness; for a man's life does not consist in the abundance of his possessions." And he told them a parable, saying, "The land of a rich man brought forth plentifully; and he thought to himself, 'What shall I do, for I have nowhere to store my crops?' And he said, 'I will do this: I will pull down my barns, and build larger ones; and there I will store all my grain and my goods. And I will say to my soul, Soul, you have ample goods laid up for many years; take your ease, eat, drink, be merry.' But God said to him, 'Fool! This night your soul is required of you; and the things you have prepared, whose will they be?' So is he who lays up treasure for himself, and is not rich toward God" (Lk 12: 13–21).

We will leave the second part for another occasion. We will now limit ourselves to considering the first few verses.

As usual, Jesus was surrounded by a lot of people. There were so many that they trampled on one another.

Imagining the scene, it isn't difficult to picture the reluctant protagonist of this episode standing in the front row because by dint of much pushing and shoving he has made his way up there, getting as close to Jesus as possible. He wanted to approach him, but, from what Saint Luke tells us, he apparently was not motivated so much by a laudable desire to hear the Lord as by selfish interests. He wanted to get something out of him for himself and was looking for the chance to make himself heard. Actually, he was not there to hear Jesus but to get Jesus to listen to him.

As soon as the Lord paused for a moment to catch his breath and before he could start to speak again, that man broke in with his selfish petition, without any consideration for the others: "Teacher, bid my brother divide the inheritance with me.'

We see that he was worried about money. Till then, the Lord had been talking about eternal life, about very important matters that we need to know in order to live our lives on earth. He had been saying that it is necessary to beware of the leaven of the Pharisees, of their hypocrisy, because there was nothing hidden that would not one day be revealed, and what was whispered in private would be shouted from the housetops. He said that it wasn't those who kill the body, and after that have no more that they can do, who are to be feared, but, rather, he who, after he has killed, has power to cast into hell. He said that even the very hairs of our head are numbered and that not a single sparrow of little worth is forgotten by God, and so, how much more would God not forget men, who are worth more than many sparrows.

All this, however, does not appear to have made much of an impression on our man. He wasn't listening because he wasn't really interested in what Jesus was saying. All the while he was thinking about his money, about the money that was his but that his brother had taken from him. He was obsessed by the thought of that money, which would be his to enjoy if he could get his hands on it. Nothing was more important to him. He couldn't think of anything else. After all, it was a matter of justice. The money by rights belonged to him as part of his inheritance. Against all law, his brother wouldn't give back what was his. He was totally in the right. Law and justice, both very necessary, were completely on his side. His brother, however, didn't see things that way and wouldn't give him his money.

Since Jesus had great authority and prestige, this man sought him for his obsessive purpose. He didn't care a bit about what was being preached, about eternal life, hell, love of neighbor, and all the rest. He didn't care to hear about anything, except justice, perhaps. For it was unjust of his brother not to give him his inheritance. Justice *is* very important.

The crowd would probably become hushed as it awaited the answer. Perhaps they would witness how a thorny problem concerning two brothers would be resolved with a few words, and then, once again, they would marvel at how Jesus made something complicated seem so simple and easy. But they were in for a surprise of a different sort. His answer was not what they had expected. Jesus, who was always so concerned about doing good, who loved to heal and console, who helped the needy and the suffering, absolutely refused to get involved.

The selfishness of the request may have annoyed him. It was so out of place. Or he may have been put off by the man's lack of consideration in treating him like a servant who could be ordered about. The tone with which the request was made, however, might have softened its harshness. In any case, Jesus did not take him up on it.

It is worthwhile to consider this answer slowly. We may well ask why Jesus, for whom it would have been so easy to do the man a favor, quite abruptly washed his hands of the entire matter. We might be surprised and even disappointed at his adamant refusal to get involved, particularly because friendship between brothers, more than money, was at stake.

It really would not have been difficult at all to do what was being asked. That is what makes us pause to reflect why he acted the way he did. Although it would have been easy to solve that man's problem, he absolutely refused to do so.

He tells us why. He had come to mediate between men and God, and between God and men, but not between men themselves, not between one set of people and another. It is important to understand this, particularly nowadays. The Word became flesh to save men from the devil's power, redeeming us from the slavery of sin. He shows us the way of salvation. He restores us to grace and friendship with God. He reveals the mysteries of the kingdom of heaven. His mission is to raise us to the supernatural world lost through Adam's sin, not to subordinate the supernatural to a fading world, with its temporal, human interests.

I want to reiterate the importance of setting this straight. We see that Jesus did not give in on this point at all. You recall what he did when some men tried to trip him up by asking whether it was licit or not to pay the tribute to Caesar. He called for a coin.

Holding it up for the Pharisees to see, he asked: "Whose likeness and inscription is this?" Caesar's, they replied. Well, then, "Render to Caesar the things that are Caesar's, and to God the things that are God's" (Mk 12: 16–17). (Incidentally, the answer put Caesar in his proper place. The inscription attributed to him the title

Pontifex maximus, that is, High Priest.) The reply disappointed the Pharisees and may have even irritated them. They would certainly have preferred to have Jesus deny the lawfulness of paying the tribute. They could then have gotten rid of him. But if he had said that the tribute was lawful, it wouldn't have made that much difference, for he would be siding with the Romans, and, in consequence, he would alienate the people and fall into public disgrace.

In fact, the Pharisees were the ones who had betrayed God's promise and their religion by using them for worldly purposes. Their opposition to Jesus started precisely when he began to repudiate their earthly messiahship and the idea of a Messiah who would come to serve only people of flesh and blood. For him, those ideas were a pale reflection of the reality he would inaugurate through grace—a new and higher life.

Thinking it over a bit, we can see how silly it would be for God to humiliate himself to the extent of taking on human nature simply to solve problems that men could solve themselves by using their God-given intelligence, good will, and patience. To be a judge between men is not much of a mission for the Son of God!

Of course this does not mean that he is not interested in us. He died for us! But he doesn't treat us like infants or incompetents. He is perfectly clear about the difference between essentials and accidentals. He did not come to alter political, social, or economic structures. He came to change man, if man wanted to be changed. He loved us to the extreme of being insulted, humiliated, spat upon, and crucified, without ever threatening those who hurt him so unjustly. He did not come to solve the problem of hunger or of housing or to do away with suffering. He himself suffered, and he did not spare those he loved from suffering. He never dealt with forms of government, except in the case of his Church, his Body, of which he is the Head. He wasn't concerned with social or economic questions. He left men to solve everything they could and should by themselves. He came to earth to solve what man, either individually or collectively, could not solve by himself. He came to teach what no man could teach and to give what no man could give. Yet his teaching helps man to live on earth, providing the ideas that can resolve all soluble problems and help us to bear manfully and fruitfully those that have no solution.

I said earlier that this is a very important point. I suppose you already know that the Church continues to carry out Christ's saving mission and bring the fruit of redemption to all until the end of time. Holy Mother Church is the New Covenant formed by those who believe in Jesus, the Son of God—those who have been baptized in the name of the Father and of the Son and of the Holy Spirit. She is the mystical Body with Christ as her Head. In addition, Jesus founded his Church to spread the Kingdom of God on earth and to direct all of creation back to the Creator, restoring that order and harmony destroyed by original sin. This evidently implies that the Church acts in the world and on the world. This is her mission. For this she was constituted and endowed with superhuman powers. You can see that the Church is no greater than her Founder, nor can she do more than he did. This seems to me to be rather easy to understand.

Yet, for some unknown reason, there are people who find it hard to grasp and difficult to accept. As happens with all truths, this one is situated between two opposite erroneous positions, whose proponents then subject it to contrary attacks. With a slight change of diction, the modern Pharisees now ask: "Should the Church get involved in the world or not?" The Catholic and Protestant liberals of the nineteenth century thought not. According to them, the Church's concern is supernatural. She has no business getting involved in human affairs. The relations between Church and state, all laws governing education, economics, and social issues, should be carefully isolated from religious contamination. This is the present position of those favoring peaceful coexistence between Christianity and Marxism. They believe that Christianity, as a religious faith, should not provide solutions or directions for the world, because the world belongs to Marxism, which has the scientific knowledge required for governing human society and the world. Consequently, they think, there can be Christian Marxists, just as there are Christian engineers. They are perfectly happy with this solution—a complete separation between the supernatural and temporal spheres, each within its own independent and incommunicable compartment.

This solution has not satisfied everyone. After the Second World War, the opposite idea came to the fore. Christianity is not for the other world but for the here and now. It is not man, but the world, that needs to be saved. Christians, they say, should "work in the world to free created reality by using it properly" in the service of mankind, for the sake of universal fraternity. The world will be freed "in community." Accordingly, the Church should not only speak out against injustice. She should actively help do away with it by giving her blessing and help to the revolutionary liberation movements, which, by and large, are directed against capitalism.

These are two contrary positions. One supports the Church's detachment from the temporal sphere. The other encourages radical engagement in the world. Whereas the first position tries to convert the Church into a disembodied spirit, the second turns her into an instrument for purely secular purposes. Both tend to destroy the Church. The first destroys her by taking away any supernatural influence in the lives of men and their society, thereby frustrating the mission for which she was constituted. The second dilutes her supernatural content, reducing it to a mere tool to be utilized for purposes having no relation to her real mission.

The second tendency now seems to be in the ascendancy. It doesn't appear openly but works behind the scenes, setting the stage, fostering its mentality among Catholics, so that when the curtain is raised, everything seems to be in its proper place.

Take, for instance, "democracy" in the Church. It is clear that the Church is hierarchical and monarchical, with a visible head, the Pope, the Vicar of Christ, who has complete authority of order and jurisdiction. The Pope governs the entire Church, while the bishops, subordinate to him, govern in their dioceses. This form of government is not the product of a human arrangement. It was established by Christ himself. If one were to deny this openly and explicitly, he would fall under excommunication, cutting himself off *ipso facto* from communion with the Church. I suppose that heretical statements from persons outside the Church have slight effect on Catholics. However, there are subtler methods, which were originally employed by the Arians and, more recently, by the Jansenists. These consist in speaking in such a way that it is always possible to stretch the words and give them an orthodox interpretation.

Cardinal Newman said that the most pernicious error springs from a corrupted truth. There are terms that, when properly understood, express correct concepts, for example, "shared responsibility," "participation," "representation," and "dialogue." Yet they can also be used in ways that express concepts distinct from what they were meant to signify. For instance, if one were to say, with reference to the Church, that "nowadays no authority can impose a law on a community unless the people themselves, either directly or indirectly, assume their role of shared responsibility in drafting laws," he, in fact, would be denying that a Pope or bishop has the faculty to make laws without first securing the agreement of, or at least consulting, those governed, on the grounds that shared responsibility demands shared decision-making. It matters little if he insists that he is not implying that the Church is a democracy, for, in his terms, either the authority makes decisions under pressure and runs the risk of not governing but simply rubber-stamping the decisions made by persons without authority, or else it resists being told what to do by any group, in which case it would be violently attacked for its action. In either case, the effect on souls is disastrous. The faithful are neglected while their leaders wrangle over policies and structures that are quite foreign to the Gospel's view of authority in the Church—"he who hears you, hears me"—and that are really only excuses to justify their lack of obedience.

The Church does not exist to solve social problems, though she may help quite effectively to find their solution. Her purpose is to teach mankind the way of salvation, providing the means to achieve that end. While she looks forward to the final resurrection and eternal life, she carries out her mission on earth among men and women who live in this tangible world. She must preach the Gospel. She must teach souls what Christ has revealed. She has to give them a Christian outlook with which they can live in all circumstances as children of God, doing their work, fulfilling their duties, and exercising their rights with the spirit that characterizes Christ's faithful. The Church does not exist to organize things on earth, though she does infuse, through the faithful, the spirit of the Gospel into the secular city, without abdicating her supernatural mission or debasing and diluting it by mediating between men and meddling in matters on which men may legitimately hold differing opinions. What the Church does is to raise man to a higher plane, so that, with greater perspective and a better will, he can solve those problems. She teaches only those dogmas which are contained in revelation and pertain exclusively to the supernatural order. How could the Church remain faithful to Christ and to her nature if she were tied to an economic or political system, officially preaching what are essentially opinions on various matters? She refrained from doing this even in the time of the Emperors Nero and Trajan.

While she instructed her faithful to obey the pagan rulers in areas where they rightfully had authority, she also taught when they had to refuse to obey. The Christians learned the lesson so well that they chose to die rather than obey when obedience to the rulers would have meant disobedience to Christ.

The Church is concerned with temporal matters only insofar as they are related to the final end of man and of creation. She then can command what is to be done and what is not to be done. She has always exercised this right. She says what is in accord with the Gospel and what is not. However, the faithful, as human beings and as citizens, living in society and earning their daily bread by the sweat of their brow, are the ones to infuse the Christian spirit into their lives and all their activities. The Church teaches what is right and wrong, licit and illicit. She teaches love of neighbor and generosity, but she does not tell the Christian to establish a republic, a monarchy, a democracy, or an aristocracy. She doesn't tell Christians to be capitalists or socialists in economics. She will, however, defend, as she always has, man's freedom to do as he sees fit in what is licit and to believe as he thinks best in non-dogmatic matters that God has left to the free opinion of men.

No Christian can compromise the Church by using her name in secular matters or asking her to back his opinions. Priests should also avoid this pitfall. They cannot use the Gospel as a sounding board to preach about politics, economics, or sociology from the pulpit or in workshops for their elites.

Although the words of the Second Vatican Council pertinent to this point are very clear, they are rarely quoted: "The specific mission Christ entrusted to his Church does not belong to the political, economic, or social order; he gave her a religious purpose." The religious order, however, is not limited to mankind alone, for all creation has been reconciled with God through Christ. Therefore, "the Church's mission is not simply to offer men Christ's message and grace, but also to infuse and perfect the entire temporal order with the spirit of the Gospel."

Give to God what is God's and to Caesar what is Caesar's. Now that clerics are so busy denouncing "structures," eliminating hunger, and improving social conditions (generally in places far removed from their parishes and cloisters), doing what civil authorities should be doing, one wonders who is concerned about teaching the catechism of *Christian* doctrine, about hearing confessions, and administering the other sacraments.

Don't become clerical. Jesus did not come to settle disputes among men. Similarly, he did not establish his Church to solve purely temporal problems. You are the ones who have to solve them. As long as you have the right ideas, you will go about this task without dragging our Mother, the Church, through thorny problems that would only tear her apart, and even, God forbid, leave her disfigured and unrecognizable.

7

Poverty as Virtue

"To him who lays up treasure for himself . . ."

When we were speaking some time ago about the episode (Lk 12: 13–21) where Jesus' preaching led someone to ask him to get his brother to divide an inheritance with him, we left aside the second, and larger, part of the text, to deal with it on another occasion. So, let's look at it now.

After making it quite clear that he was not going to interfere in this kind of thing, Jesus tried to help that poor man, obsessed with money, by opening up a whole new vista. "A man's life does not consist in the abundance of his possessions," he told him. He went on to tell the parable about the man who had a great harvest and, when he saw it coming, began to think what he would do with it, and then he hit on an ideal solution: he would tear down his barns and build larger ones and store up all his wealth: "'And I will say to my soul, Soul, you have ample goods laid up for many years; take your ease, eat, drink, be merry.' But God said to him, 'Fool! This night your soul is required of you; and the things you have prepared, whose will they be?' So is he who lays up treasure for himself, and is not rich toward God" (Lk 12:19–21).

Yes: in the light of the most decisive and important event in a man's life—his death—what use is wealth, anyway? Eternal life is not a reward given to those who have best proven their abilities to store up material wealth, which they cannot enjoy indefinitely; it is not a reward given to those who are not rich in God's eyes.

There is a different kind of wealth, which one does not leave behind when one dies; a wealth, in fact, which one discovers only when death comes on the scene. In the last analysis, what is the point of spending one's life piling up one million on top of another, when in the end one is buried just with the clothes one has on? Money is of no use to a dead man, nor are any of the things money can buy. Life, eternal life, does not consist in property. It does not even consist in temporal, earthly life. Rich people, even the richest people, end up dying.

I'm afraid that in today's world a Catholic can find this point quite disconcerting. If my memory serves me rightly, Papini, an Italian writer, referred to money as "Satan's dung"; but obviously even Papini* could not have got by without having some money. Saint Francis of Assisi wanted his followers not even to touch money, but Jesus and his disciples did use money to provide themselves with the necessities of life. On the other hand, there is no doubt about the fact that the Gospel preaches poverty and says such strange things as this: "Woe to you that are rich, for you have received your consolation" (Lk 6: 24); and goes so far as to state categorically that it is more difficult for a rich man to enter the kingdom of heaven than for a camel to pass through the eye of a needle (see Mt 19: 24).

No one could say that the way of the world is in line with the Gospel teaching on poverty. In fact, it seems to be going in the opposite direction; shortly after he became Pope, Paul VI spoke about the spirit of poverty, to which the Gospel gives such importance, and said it was being "threatened by the value present-day outlook gives to (material) things." It is easy enough to see that this is the case. Nowadays, economics seems to occupy the number

---

* Giovanni Papini (1881–1956), prolific Italian novelist, poet, historian, and author of books on philosophy and theology. His lifework fills 65 volumes.

one position, which means that greater values, much greater values, are being relegated to second, third, or last place; and this bodes ill. Everyone is talking nowadays about "the standard of living." People are evaluated in terms, not of what they *are*, but of what they *have*; and the saying "A man is worth what he has" is perhaps truer today than ever it was. People are being evaluated as if they were objects: "Do you see so-and-so? He is worth millions." When people are measured in terms of money, it means that they have become "things": they are things that have their price and can be bought.

In the world today, wealth, money that can be used to acquire things as luxurious as they are useless, entertainment as expensive as it is anti-Christian, appearances as dear as they are empty; for very many people this is the great aim; they go crazy in a tireless search to create new needs to market new things and accumulate more money.

It is in this very world, hung up on money, that for some years now a kind of new wind of purification and austerity seems to be blowing in certain Christian sectors, aimed at cleansing the Church and the world of riches. The expression "The Church of the poor" is, it seems to me, designed to counteract the contamination that is supposed to have affected the Church and aims at restoring evangelical austerity.

It sounds good, but difficulties begin to arise when you start asking what does this expression (Church of the poor) actually mean? Who are the poor? Should the rich be excluded from the Church? In the Gospel we find rich people who are, not only good, but even so good (for example, the father of the prodigal son) that they are used to give us some idea of how good God is toward sinners or who are so detached from things (like Zacchaeus) that they give away a lot of their money as soon as they come to know Jesus. We also find poor people, like the man who wanted his brother to share the inheritance with him, whose heart was so eaten up with greed that Jesus invented in his honor the parable about the rich man with the great harvest. Benedict Joseph Labre was a beggar, Saint Ferdinand was a king, Saint Agnes was a rich woman, Saint Peter of Alcantara had nothing at all. They were all saints.

It would seem that up to now the poverty of "the Church of the poor" refers mainly or exclusively to the liturgy. People want to get rid of ostentation, waste, and luxury. I don't exactly know what ostentation, or luxury, in religious worship means. Would it refer to a monstrance (for exposition of the Blessed Sacrament) that contains precious stones or to a rich tabernacle? Perhaps the point is that a ruby or a sapphire is better when worn by a woman at some society event than when used in a chalice that is designed to contain the Blood of Christ, or maybe the precious stone should be kept in a bank vault, under lock and key. A bishop's staff made of wood can be dearer than one made of metal, and vestments that appear to be quite primitive may in fact be more expensive than others that seem richer. Once upon a time this happened: a woman broke an alabaster flask containing a very expensive perfume, which she used to anoint Jesus. Only one disciple, Judas, in fact, objected: Why was this ointment not sold—it would have fetched three hundred denarii—and the money given to the poor? Saint John, who was present and who had known Judas for some time, commented in his Gospel, "This he said, not because he cared for the poor but because he was a thief, and as he had the money box he used to take what was put into it." What is of interest to us now, however, is not so much Saint John's comment as Jesus' reaction: "Let her alone, let her keep it for the day of my burial. The poor you always have with you, but you do not always have me" (Jn 12:6–8). Besides, I don't think that anyone with even an average knowledge of the history of the Church can be unaware that if there is anyone who has shown real concern to alleviate the position of the poor it has been the Church, in all ages.

In particular, I believe, as someone wrote not so long ago, that "beautiful things, even if costly, can be put to no better purpose in this world than here" (in the liturgy). A church is God's house, but it is also the home of his children. And it is the only place where the poorest of them, in the same comfort and to the same degree as the rich, can enjoy the beauties of art, the splendor of the liturgy, the wonders from which they are barred elsewhere. And all that beauty is also theirs, even though they have not paid for it with their money, and they share in it with the same right as the most wealthy of the faithful.

In any event, what I wanted to say was that when we talk about poverty, we should use the word in the Christian sense, that is to say, in an evangelical sense. And to do this we need to reflect on a few more things, because if we do not we run the risk of playing with ambiguous concepts, mixing things up and ending up in a "dialogue of the deaf," in which no one understands anything because everyone has his own idea of what poverty means without ever checking whether this idea is or is not Gospel-based.

Man has certain needs. God put him in the world, and he also endowed the world with resources to meet those needs. Therefore, the possession of some material resources is something everyone needs. These resources—which are good things—are only means, not ends; and they are means God gives man in order to enable him to attain the goal for which he was created. When all is said and done, man has to attain his supernatural goal. Man has to make his way on earth, and to do this he cannot live on air. Therefore, we must get two ideas clear at the very start: the things of the earth are not bad, they are good; they exist to help man reach his natural goal and his supernatural goal. And there is a third idea we need to bring in: absolutely speaking, it is not men who have created the earth's resources, but God. Strictly speaking, they are *his*, and he gives them to men for a specific purpose. This amounts to saying that, so far as these resources are concerned, we are simply managers of them—and we will one day have to render an account of the use we have made of them.

Money is merely a thing. So is a cottage in the country, a beach house, a car, a bottle of wine, a tree, a painting, or a violin. These are material goods; and in addition to them there are also spiritual goods—art, music, poetry, and so on. Both of these kinds of resources exist for man, the lord of creation; but they are still only things and cannot be put into moral categories of "good" or "evil." As beings—"ontologically"—they are good, because everything is good; but morally they are indifferent (that is, neither good nor bad) because they are mere things.

After that introduction, I think we now have some basis on which to develop the subject. If you read the Gospel, you will see that neither Jesus nor Mary lived in indigence, nor were they beggars; Jesus did not preach that misery was a virtue or that it was good for a person to lack an indispensable minimum. Nor did he say anything about there being any need to divide things equally among everyone. He preached poverty or, to put it more accurately, the *virtue* of poverty, but he was not a demagogue or someone with a chip on his shoulder who would save the poor just because they were poor or condemn the wealthy because they owned things. He aimed at a much deeper, much more radical, level: "Where your treasure is, there will your heart be also" (Mt 7: 21). Did he not tell us that what stains a man is not what comes from outside? What stains a man is what comes from his heart. The goods of this world are things external to man; and because he cannot totally do without them, the fact of having enough to enable one to reach one's natural and supernatural goals does not go against poverty. If it did, poverty could not be preached as a virtue that, because it is evangelical, is obligatory for everyone. Someone as above suspicion as Saint Thomas Aquinas (he is a Doctor of the Church, remember) goes so far as to assert that "it is impossible to practice the virtue [of poverty] if one does not have a minimum of material well-being." If this minimum is lacking, then it is almost impossible for man even to reach his natural goal, because he is always at risk of descending into an instinctive and almost animal struggle to stay alive, unable to think about anything other than self-preservation.

The goods of the earth, wealth, money—these are means that make sense only in connection with the purpose for which they exist. When man stops seeing them as means and turns them into ends, he stops being poor. When a man becomes a slave of money, when he devotes his time and his best efforts to acquiring more and more wealth, then he has become rich. His heart is possessed by money: riches become his treasure. "A person who loves God," Saint Augustine said, "cannot love money," and he explained: "I am not saying that he may not love money, but that he must not have *much* love for it." When a person gets attached to money, when greed or avarice finds its way into his soul, he has ceased to serve God and has entered the service of an idol. "Use money," Saint Augustine went on, "as a wayfarer who stops at an

inn uses a table, a glass, a plate, a bed—with the intention of leaving it, not of staying there."

Things, money included, are there only to be used.
Yes, but how are we to use them? Bearing in mind man's
purpose—to give glory to God and thereby attain salvation—things (which mean little or nothing in themselves) take on importance in the degree to which they
help to give God glory and make for men's salvation;
their usefulness should be measured in terms of what
they contribute to that aim, and one should never forget
that he has to leave them behind. It is not that there is
anything wrong with earning money. What is wrong is
not to give away readily what one does not need or to
store money up for one's own benefit and to use it to
accumulate more and more things, ever more superflu-
ous things, that a rich man can hardly enjoy because he
spends all his time trying to get more money in order to
keep up an ever more affluent lifestyle, spending more
and more money on more and more useless things. I
know it is difficult for human selfishness to practice what
Saint Thomas says we should do: "As far as the enjoyment of external goods is concerned, man should *not*
possess them *as if* they were exclusively his own, but *as if*
they were common property for the use of himself and
others, in such a way that everyone places them at the
disposal of others to meet their needs." However, it is
possible to act like this when, with a truly Christian
spirit, we regard wealth not as a possession but as a form
of service, as something that enables us to come to the
aid of our neighbor.

The modern world's obsession with money involves
certain disadvantages. Earning more in order to have
more, spending time and energy to get one's hands on
even a tiny bit of all the money in circulation, living at
an ever more expensive level—this absorbs almost all

of one's available time, in such a way that many men—more and more, I fear—cannot properly look after their children or even their wives, and their home becomes just a kind of lodging house where they sleep, that is, when they are not away on business. And then there is the whole entourage that money involves in terms of social engagements and business relationships, which consume the little time left over—time that should be for rest or for leisurely friendship—because one has no leisure, and friendship does not need all this carry-on.

At the other extreme, there are those who are forever preaching poverty, those who profess to be scandalized by everything they regard as a lack of poverty, those who thunder against the rich and say nice things about the poor. These people give me the impression that they are preaching an ostentatious and artificial poverty, to attract attention. A person who is really poor does not talk so much; still less does he exhibit his poverty as something exemplary that pleases him no end.

Being poor is not itself a virtue, Saint Bernard used to say but, rather, love of poverty is. A poor person who is full of anger because he does not have what others have is really a rich man at heart. Evangelical poverty is something different: it is detachment, it is having one's heart free of the burden that attachment to money, to earthly things, involves: "In any and all circumstances I have learned the secret of facing plenty and hunger, abundance and want," Saint Paul wrote.

It was all the same to him: it had no effect on him. The spirit of poverty means understanding that we are managers of resources that belong to God and that we have to render an account to him of the use we make, good or bad, of these things entrusted to our care for the benefit of others. It means being content with what is enough and, instead of creating ever new and more expensive needs,

giving away what we don't need. The state tries to improve the lot of its weaker members, of the poorer citizens, and tries to bring about a more just distribution of
wealth, but this does not exempt him who has from coming to the aid of people in need. It is too easy to take refuge
in the state or to say that almsgiving humiliates the poor.
Apart from the fact that a truly poor person never feels
humiliated when a generous-hearted person gives him a
hand, it all depends on the spiritual elegance of the giver
or the lack of it: whether he gives the way someone
throws a scrap to a dog or shares something with his
brother. In the last analysis, a person *has*, not what he does
not need or accumulate but, rather, what he *gives*. It is a
question, don't forget, of being rich in the eyes of God. It
is easy to talk a lot about poverty: anyone can do it. Nor
does it cost anything to think about the poor. The difficult
thing is to be detached, to give away what one does not
need, to avoid creating new needs, to stop comparing oneself with one's neighbor and feeling small because he has
more, being content at having a smaller wage when one is
worth (in one's own eyes) so much more, and adjusting to
having fewer material goods.

I also think that evangelical poverty has quite a lot to
do with work. I think it was Gratry who defined poverty
as "acquiring through work what one needs for daily
life." And Saint Paul said, "For even when we were with
you, we gave you this command: If any one will not
work, let him not eat. For we hear that some of you are
living in idleness, mere busybodies, not doing any work.
Now such persons we command and exhort in the Lord
Jesus Christ to do their work in quietness and to earn
their own living" (2 Thess 3: 10–12): One might say that
that person is poor who lives from his work, who earns
what he eats, whose capital—the best kind of capital—is
his daily effort. And I think that person has the greater

spirit of poverty who, using the resources available to improve his position, lives at the level his income permits, rather than the person who spends more than he earns and is forever complaining about how difficult it is to make ends meet.

Money is not the only thing. One's family—one's wife and children—also has rights. And so does God. Rest, a minimum of rest, is also necessary, because life must not become endless business (negotiation, Lat. *nec-otium*, no rest); man must not become a robot, a *homo faber*, a mere worker. The virtue of poverty works to keep man free from being controlled by external things—to prevent any of these things from chaining him, making a slave of him, and separating him from God. There is no point in arriving at the moment of death with a load of useless junk and with our hands empty of supernatural goods.

When a man makes money his primary objective, he is trapped. But remember this: evangelical poverty does not consist in having or not having but, rather, in being detached, as Saint Josemaría reminds us in *The Way*. And a beggar can be as avaricious or as greedy as any very rich man. Avarice and greed are not caused by externals: they arise in the heart, and every heart is basically the same: it can go whichever way one chooses to let it.

I would not like to think that you have chosen as your goal what seems to be the objective of quite a few young people nowadays: coming out on top, achieving notoriety and money. I would rather like to see you planning to serve God and others by means of your work and being generous toward those who have less than you or nothing at all. Everything else will be given you besides. Do what you ought to do. And in the matter of poverty and riches, what you should do—what we disciples of Christ, we Christians—should do is not to treasure up money but to share with others what we have. Giving food to the hungry, clothing the naked, communicating what we know to those who don't know, lending a book to someone who doesn't have one because he cannot afford to buy it or even making him a present of it—in other words, making ourselves rich in God's eyes. When you think about it, you don't really need all that much, as that poor man in Assisi showed us centuries ago, and as yesterday's hippies could have shown—but instead of merely shedding useless baggage they equipped themselves with even more useless stuff.

"Don't forget it: he has most who needs least. Don't create needs for yourself" (*The Way*, no. 630). Good advice, and it goes to the heart of the virtue of poverty preached by Christ. Don't let yourself become a slave of anything; use things only insofar as you need them, no more. Give away what you don't need, help everyone you can, and, for the love of God, don't let money, even the money you have to cover your expenses and entertainment, get a grip on you so you become like that man who wanted the share of the inheritance. Great wealth engenders great longings, Donoso Cortés, the nineteenth-century Spanish thinker, said. I know that you young people are not greedy or avaricious . . . yet. But if you become accustomed to indulging your whims, create ever greater needs, and spend what you have not yet earned, then you are on the slippery slope; if you really want to reform a society that is meaningless, begin by living in a poor way, that is to say, soberly. Not by an ostentatious kind of poverty, a trumpeted poverty, which accuses society of being corrupted by money but, rather, in a way whereby your right hand does not know what your left hand is doing. And by working, because no one has a right to be a burden on others if he can avoid it.

And forgive me if I say that, in general, my impression is that young people today are not distinguished by their sobriety and their spirit of poverty. My reading leads me to think that they have more money than ever and spend more than ever. They also have more needs than ever before. Businessmen were, I think, the first to see this, and they began very early on to zero in on the youth market. I don't know whether you keep an account of your expenses; I do know that poor people do, and they stretch their money and watch every penny because they don't have very much and it took them all their time to earn it. So, until you understand how much effort it takes to earn money, until you have to make sure you can stretch your money to meet your needs, and until you experience doing without something in order to help others, you have not yet grasped the spirit of poverty proper to a Christian.

Until we live like that, I don't think we have any right to protest about hunger in the world or about under-development or about all those things that are so much in fashion—or to think that we have a Christian spirit because we go to Mass on Sunday and say nice things in favor of the poor.

8

The Sacrament of Penance

"Your sins are forgiven you."

A paralytic once heard Jesus say these words to him. Some friends, perhaps, or relatives had carried him from his bed to our Lord in Capernaum. But there was such a crowd milling about the house in which Jesus was speaking that they couldn't get inside. Instead, they lowered him through the roof into the room where Jesus was. When Christ saw him and the faith of his friends, he said to the paralytic: "My son, your sins are forgiven."

As usual, the scribes and Pharisees present began to murmur within themselves: "It is blasphemy! Who can forgive sins but God alone?" Then Jesus, seeing their thoughts, spoke to them, saying: "Which is easier, to say to the paralytic, 'Your sins are forgiven,' or to say, 'Rise, take up your pallet and walk'? But that you may know that the Son of man has authority on earth to forgive sins. . . ."

They saw it all with their own eyes. Only downright fanaticism could blind them to the facts. That is what happened, even when the paralytic, in obedience to Jesus' command, took up his stretcher and instantly began to walk.

Leaving aside other interesting aspects that Saint Mark presents in this passage (2:1–12), I would like to focus on this chief idea: only God can forgive sins. That this is true derives from the fact that sin is essentially an offense against God and, of course, only an offended party can forgive an injury. A careful reading of Saint

Mark's text shows that Jesus came to declare clearly that he was God precisely because he could forgive sins. The miracle was simply the means he used to try to help people see this truth.

Perhaps we all have thought at times that this is a wonderful way to be forgiven, particularly as the paralytic said nothing. But this is not Jesus' usual way of forgiving. He left us baptism, which forgives all our sins without our having to accuse ourselves of anything specific. This is a great gift. Since, however, no one is confirmed in the state of grace in this life, any sin after baptism costs us God's grace and friendship. Knowing full well how weak and fragile we are, the Lord left us, in addition, the sacrament of penance so we could pick ourselves up every time we fall. Some treatises on moral theology call penance "the second chance." If we sin after baptism, we can keep from drowning by grabbing on to confession. But there is no other lifesaver if we spurn the sacrament of penance.

This is neither the time nor place to go extensively into the theology of confession. For more details you can read the *Instruction on Penance* of the Congregation of the Faith (June 1972).* Instead, I would like to make some comments that might be useful in view of present-day attempts to force the Church to change her regulations concerning this sacrament. At this late date, none of us can be surprised to learn that there is a persistent campaign to convince the faithful that individual confession of serious sins is not required to receive absolution.

Don't get your hopes up that rules governing this sacrament will be relaxed so the faithful will no longer have to undergo the humiliation of telling their sins. Individual accusation of sins is essential to the sacra-

* If Father Suarez were writing today, he would refer to more recent documents of the Magisterium, including the *Catechism of the Catholic Church.*

ment as defined by the Council of Trent—something that has always been the teaching and practice of the Church. Don't be scandalized, as some are nowadays, at the mention of Trent. It was a great council, which defined some important doctrinal matters. Those definitions are so precise that they cannot be changed, even by the Pope, with all his spiritual authority as the Vicar of Christ. According to theologians, dogmatic declarations of an ecumenical council, once approved by the Pope, limit the further exercise of papal infallibility, because they are themselves infallible. To say that the Pope is infallible certainly does not mean that he can teach whatever he wants. And let us not forget that Vatican Council II borrowed heavily from Trent, despite the efforts of some people to misrepresent the most recent of ecumenical councils.

Unfortunately, the Church is being pressured to change what cannot be changed, while the faithful are being bombarded with the same deceitful propaganda. We are being asked to get excited over the latest proposal that would liberate us from whatever goes against our pride or comfort. For your own sake, don't pay attention to that clerical-sociological literature which parades as theological learning. It might sound deep and spiritual, it might claim to be a pastorally motivated return to the beginnings, but if you scratch the surface you will discover serious errors, propagated to keep the faithful away from confession.

For example: "Reconciliation takes place in the community," because "it is in the community that forgiveness comes from God and is transmitted through the priest, who represents the community." Since when? Who said so? With such verbiage people try to shame us out of the practice of individual confession by appeals to our base tendencies. The traditional practice of confession, for certain people, bespeaks psychological immaturity and represents a spiritual trauma. We are told that confession depersonalizes the sacramental relationship and does away with the Church community. I spare you the rest. What could be more personal than to acknowledge your own infidelities in the confessional? And what is so personal about a collective penitential rite, in which participants hide their sins?

We all must learn to maneuver our way through these treacherous waters. No matter how often you hear or read that the general confession at the beginning of Mass or the prayers at a penitential service (even when followed by collective absolution from a priest) suffice to forgive serious sins, don't believe it. The substitutes may be attractive and painless, but by themselves they are as effective in forgiving mortal sins as aspirin is for curing a broken leg. I don't know who is directing the chorus of voices intent on attacking the sacrament of penance in the name of new communal formulas, but they are all singing the same hypnotic tune. We can easily be taken in; our pride and selfishness would welcome an easy way out. That is why we need an authoritative voice to tell us the truth and to warn us of error. But, unfortunately, today few voices are raised to expose these hucksters of a new way.

Let us review our catechism. Confession, that is, the secret and personal self-accusation of *all* mortal sins committed since the last valid confession, is necessary for the forgiveness of sins. All serious sins have to be told in number and species with the circumstances that modify the species (stealing an ordinary object worth two hundred dollars, for example, is not the same sin as stealing a chalice worth the same amount). Of course, there are cases when the Church dispenses one from this serious obligation of personal confession, but they are very limited exceptions. For instance, a priest can give collective absolution, without individual accusation of sins, to passengers of an airplane about to crash or on a boat about to sink or to a dying man, about to breathe his last, who makes some sign of contrition. But, even then, if the passengers (or soldiers) survive the catastrophe or recover from the brink of death, they are bound to make a complete confession to a priest in the ordinary way if they wish to have their sins forgiven. (And the same holds true for the altogether exceptional cases of collective absolution contemplated in the latest *Instruction on Penance.*)

Perhaps you might object that, in spite of everything, personal confession is not required. Doesn't an act of perfect contrition wipe out all the sins that would otherwise be told to the priest? That is true, but only if there is contrition, and perfect contrition at that. Let me try to explain.

If you have read Graham Greene's novel *Brighton Rock*, you may recall the hero, Pinkie (if I'm not mistaken), a young, lower-class gang leader and a Catholic. When he is attacked by a rival gang, he manages to hide in a garage. He knows that if he is found he'll be killed. Because he has not forgotten everything he learned as a child, he prepares to die by trying to make an act of contrition. But every time he starts to do so, he's distracted by a noise, by someone's voice. Finally, he manages to concentrate. When he gets to the part, "but most of all because I have offended you, who are all good and deserving of all my love," he hears a small voice inside saying: "You're a liar. What you really are afraid of is being condemned to hell. That's only attrition, and that's not good enough." Time goes by, and finally he's able to leave the garage. He's happy because he wasn't killed, but still he can't make an act of perfect contrition.

The moral of the story is very practical. Contrition presupposes a great love for God. It is sorrow for having harmed someone who loves us, who gave his life for us. We are sorry because, in a moment of thoughtlessness or weakness, we offend God, whom we still love. But when a person habitually ignores God or pays him scant attention, is it likely that when he suddenly finds himself in a jam he will be capable of authentic love for God, sorrow of love, contrition? Unless there is a special grace from God, it is highly unlikely. And who can be certain that God will bail him out precisely at that moment? Furthermore, contrition involves considerably more than merely reciting the Act of Contrition. It is not a magical abracadabra. Either the words sincerely express an interior attitude or they are just meaningless sounds.

For sins to be forgiven, moreover, contrition must be perfect. And we are not perfectly contrite unless we have firmly resolved to confess our serious sins to a priest as soon as possible. If our sorrow is sufficiently great to win God's forgiveness, it will certainly lead us to confess our sins in the proper manner. Dozens of acts of contrition are to no avail if we have access to a priest and do not avail ourselves of his ministry. How can we be truly sorry for having offended God if we spurn the sacramental means he has given us to return to his good graces? Only when it is impossible to go to confession can a person, after making an Act of Contrition, receive Holy Communion without having first confessed his sins, and then only when there is a grave need to receive the Eucharist. Otherwise it is better to wait. (I get the impression that some people want to appear to be in the state of grace without suffering the humiliation of admitting their faults. To me this doesn't seem like fair play. If you think it out carefully, I'm sure you'll agree.)

Redemption wins back for us graces we have lost, but it does not change our nature. By original sin, man rejected a free gift. After the redemption, man must desire, love, and obtain that gift if he wants to possess it again. The gift is available, within our reach, but we have to approach it and stretch out our hand to grasp it. Adam found it within himself, but we do not. No. God grants the gift of grace (if I may express it so) only with man's permission, which means that man can positively reject it or, without going that far, refrain from making the slightest attempt to receive it. He can also want it so earnestly that he is ready to pay any price to get it.

Permit me to clarify my point with a comparison that, while perhaps not ideal, may offer some insights. Imagine a man at the bottom of a deep pit that has sides so smooth that it is absolutely impossible for him to climb out by himself. He could, of course, cry for help. He could also sit down and simply study his insect companions or the shadows cast by the sun or moon. But if he really wants to get out, he'll call for help. And if help comes, it will probably be in the form of a rope. And even then he would have to tie the rope around his body, grasp it firmly with both hands, getting bruised in the process, and push himself up with his feet against the uncooperative walls of the pit, repeating the attempt every time he slips. If he doesn't ask for help or refuses it when it is offered, or if he stops trying when the first difficulty appears, or if he gives up at the first setback, then his interest in getting out of the darkness of the pit into daylight is dubious at best. Otherwise, he would risk suffering whatever difficulties and hardships were required.

The sacrament of confession is like the rope. It seems that the uneasiness people feel today arises from the humiliation of having to show their own wretchedness, even if only to the priest in the sacrament. Might this not be the real trouble? I have often asked myself why it is thought to be a humiliation to tell one's sins to the priest, whereas no one feels humiliated in telling those same things, and even one's dreams, in much greater detail, to a psychiatrist or psychologist. Besides, don't you see that where there is little or no faith or no recourse to this sacrament, psychiatrists are in great demand?

Saint Teresa, in her simple and wise way, without any complication or pomposity, has an explanation. She says that every soul, no matter how holy, needs an outlet. Confession is so human. It brings into the open what is shut up inside, causing oppressiveness, anxiety, or torment. Nothing is more oppressive or gives rise to more anxiety and torment than sin, because sin is disorder, a lie, evil itself. Psychologists and psychoanalysts may enable their patients to sublimate, explain away, or otherwise overcome their complexes, but all of them together cannot forgive a single sin or lift it from a patient's soul.

The reason the sacrament provokes a reaction of shame in a patient is that it brings man's evil face-to-face with God's holiness, his infinite goodness. In confession, evil is owned up to and placed before God; while in the psychiatric consultation, the same evil is first brought before another human being. In the sacrament, evil *is* monstrous; but outside that context, it very often *appears* to be merely a natural phenomenon, related not to God but, rather, to what other men do and accept.

Accordingly, personal confession of sins is itself an act of penance and the beginning of reparation. To have to go to a priest, bow one's head, swallow pride and self-love, and accuse oneself of sins, one by one, is an expression of sincere and true hatred of sin. Doubtless it is humiliating, but let's not exaggerate the discomfort. Besides, it is only right and therapeutic for this to happen.

Sin is always an act of pride and selfishness. It is an act of pride, because in disobeying and offending God the sinner imitates both the devil, who refused to serve his Creator, and Adam, who, wanting to be like God, refused to accept his inferior station. Sin is selfish, because the sinner seeks his own satisfaction, turning his back on the ensuing harm. (Every sin always harms others, even though the effects may not be perceptible, for sin increases the amount of evil in the world.) Therefore, it is only just that the sinner experience humiliation and difficulty. Humiliation cures pride and hardship our easy-going selfishness.

The humiliation surrounding confession is not that great. Once one tells one's sins, confession stops smarting and becomes a source of joy. The shame in confessing one's sins arises, among other reasons, from having to descend from one's prideful pedestal and lose face before others (although one tends to exaggerate both). That is the extent of the humiliation that, in any case, enables us to get up and start over again. Confession soon turns to exultation, because we have set things right: whoever loses should pay. So, once the debt is paid, we can again proceed on the way to God, free of burdens and light of heart.

The sinner approaches the sacrament of penance with death in his soul; there he nails to the Cross of Christ the deadly weight that annihilates all joy; and he leaves restored to eternal life. Only a person who has experienced a good confession knows what contentment and joy await the penitent. Only such a person knows what it is to pass from darkness to light, from death to life. In this sense the words of Lope de Vega are especially true: "Today I am born again, because who can exist without God?"

More than once I have had occasion to admire the

courage of people who, free of self-pity, recounted to me in confession their sins, one by one, with great clarity (and sometimes much effort). They accused themselves with the conviction of one who knows he is guilty. On the other hand, I have not been terribly impressed by those who may say the same things, but in a vague way, to the accompaniment of mitigating explanations, excuses, and rationalizations. But I am absolutely unimpressed by those who avoid being humilitated by trying to convince themselves that confession is now passé, a relic of our unenlightened past. They are like those who put off going to confession in the vain hope that one day the Church will dispense them of this bothersome procedure. They simply refuse to take responsibility for their actions, feeling excused by psychological or social conditions; or they will not admit that anything that seems good to them could be sinful.

I understand that confession is not a pleasant business, except for those who take God's sanctity seriously. In that case, the love of God spurs them on to wash away the stains, however minute they be, and to purify themselves with the blood of Christ. I must also add that frequent confession, even when there are no serious sins, is not a game or a mania for the professionally devout. If purity of soul is our aim, to continue our analogy, we want to be free, not only from big stains, but also from spots and any offensive odors. Not all who participated in Christ's Passion crucified him. Some only slapped him or spat on his face or insulted and mocked him or beat him with a reed. But you'll agree that they all contributed to his suffering. If, let us say, a mortal sin is like crucifying Christ, a deliberate venial sin is equivalent to a slap. But that hurts, too. And you can't hide behind "I haven't hurt anyone," because, as Cardinal Newman said, not to do good is really to do evil. By definition, evil is the absence of good where good should exist. Let us never forget that we also sin, and sometimes seriously, by omissions.

I have the impression that this chapter hasn't been very pleasant, and I'm sorry about that. In any case, I want you to understand that I didn't intend to frighten anyone, though God forbid that I should falsify truth in order not to upset you and spoil the enjoyment of your youth. Don't you think that a bit of a fright in time is better than a series of pious lies (which wouldn't convince you anyway)? It would be much more comfortable for me to leave you to die like pagans or to put off speaking straightforwardly to you until there is little time or strength left to rectify your life.

In Luis de Granada's *Guide for Sinners*, I read a quotation from Saint Isidore that makes a lot of sense and gives food for thought: "Whoever wants to be assured of forgiveness at the hour of his death should do penance when he is in good health, weeping for his sins. For if he has done wrong and does penance at the hour of death, he takes a great risk. Just as his condemnation is uncertain, so is his salvation doubtful."

These are strong words, which may seem harsh. But, as Saint Augustine says, putting off doing penance (in the sense of repentance) until we can no longer sin may not mean that we have left off sinning but that sins have left us. Have we stopped sinning because we willed to do so or merely because it is no longer possible for us to sin? Conversion to God may not be motivated out of love for God but occasioned by bodily weakness.

Forgiveness of sin is not a joking matter, I assure you, because our eternal destiny is at stake. Can you think of anything more serious? Only God can forgive sins, and he has entrusted that power to the Church: "If you forgive the sins of any, they are forgiven; and if you retain the sins of any, they are retained" (Jn 20:23). For God's sake and for the good of your own soul, listen to Jesus, who speaks through the infallible teaching authority of his Church. Only the Church can legitimately and authentically interpret the word of God, which is the only word that can save. What cannot save is the talk of people who teach something other than the Church's doctrine. They cannot save you, no matter how full they are of sociology, psychology, or apparent pastoral concern.

9

Love and Sexuality

"Like angels in heaven . . ."

The Pharisees were not the only ones to put complicated questions to Jesus to try to trap him in his speech. Sometimes the Sadducees gave them a hand. The Sadducees, another of the influential Jerusalem cliques, did not believe in the resurrection of the dead. As they saw it, everything began and ended here on earth. As you can imagine, with that outlook they were not ones to go in for asceticism and penance, and they tended to be seen as people who adapted themselves to circumstances, always managing to turn them to their own advantage. They did not worry much about obeying the precepts and traditions of the elders, nor did they go in for rigorous interpretation of the law; they even got on quite well with the Romans, having none of the nationalistic zeal of the Pharisees.

Although they were not so interested in Jesus' teaching as were the Pharisees, they nevertheless wanted a piece of the action from time to time. And because one of the points on which they differed most with the Pharisees had to do with the resurrection, they geared their question to Jesus on this. Here is Saint Mark's account (12: 18–23): "And Sadducees came to him, who say that there is no resurrection; and they asked him a question, saying, 'Teacher, Moses wrote for us that if a man's brother dies and leaves a wife, but leaves no child, the man must take the wife, and raise up children for his brother. There were seven brothers; the first took a wife, and when he died left no children; and the second took her, and died, leaving no children; and the third likewise; and the seven left no children. Last of all the woman also died. In the resurrection whose wife will she be? For the seven had her as wife.'"

Notice that they do not directly ask: Is there or is there not a resurrection of the dead? They simply pose a theoretical case to show the complications that would arise if the dead did in fact rise again—as if to undermine the Lord's authority (and incidentally the Pharisees') by describing an amusing situation, the mere idea of which makes you laugh. The Pharisees, for all their limitations, had more depth and were more inclined to take serious things seriously.

Jesus replied to both points—the question put to him (the specific case, let's call it), and the implied question (about the resurrection). But we shall concern ourselves with his reply to the first question, because I think that what he says will lead us to reflect on a subject that is very topical nowadays—an important subject, even though it is given far too much importance, to the point of being at times an obsession.

We shall take Jesus' reply from Saint Luke's account (20:34–36): "And Jesus said to them, 'The sons of this age marry and are given in marriage; but those who are accounted worthy to attain to that age and to the resurrection from the dead neither marry nor are given in marriage, for they cannot die any more, because they are equal to angels and are sons of God, being sons of the resurrection.'"

"This age" refers to this world, which is mortal and impermanent, and "that age" refers to the next world, where there will be no more death, no end to eternal life. Apparently, there is a type of human relationship whose purpose and meaning are connected only with the reproduction of life, in line with the conditions laid down by God in creation and in view of the ultimate goal assigned to mankind and this world.

This ultimate goal is the resurrection. When death can no longer occur, then men will not take wives or women husbands, because human reproduction will no longer serve any purpose. But, in this world, so long as death is a fact, the human race needs to perpetuate itself; that is why there are the two sexes—God devised sex as the way new lives would come into being. And this process will continue until the number of the elect has been made up: once that has happened, there will be no world any more, and the things that were before will become things of the past. The pleasure that is associated with sexual intercourse between man and woman is, therefore, not an end in itself—just as the pleasure of taste has no purpose once we have satisfied our hunger or thirst. We could say that pleasure is a kind of incentive designed to help nature achieve its purpose.

But this purpose—so far as sexual pleasure is concerned—can be attained only in the context of marriage. Jesus is, in fact, referring to marriage, not simply to any type of sexual liaison between man and woman. A human person is not an animal, and children are not like cubs, for example, able to fend for themselves a few days after being born. When a human person is born, he has various needs, which can be looked after only by parents, in the context of a stable home life. It is not only physical needs that have to be met. Children have to learn everything, from how to speak to how to reason and think coherently. It takes years and a lot of dedication to turn a baby into a fully developed man or woman; and this calls for plenty of love, because children usually give a lot of trouble, and sometimes they are veritable tyrants. Obviously it is not difficult to love them, particularly when they are the fruit of their parents' love; in which case, they are the very personification of that love. When that is not the case, when children are an undesired by-product, merely the result of carelessness in sexual intercourse, sometimes they are not loved sufficiently, and it has even been said that, instead of bringing up children for heaven, candidates for juvenile delinquency are being produced.

Marriage is the union of a man and a woman until death them do part. People who are married are joined together by a bond only death can untie, because what God has joined together no one can put asunder. In fact, marriage is primordially ordained to reproduction, that is, to children, to such an extent that if a man and a woman were to marry with the intention of not ever having children (but without renouncing the marriage act), then that marriage would be null or, more correctly, there would be no marriage at all.

So you can see that, if the sexual relationship is denied its proper purpose, it ceases to have any meaning.

"Erotic desire," it has been said, "is a passion that produces nothing." Outside of marriage, a sexual relationship is nothing more than a simple desire to possess someone or to obtain physical pleasure. And it is *nothing* because it is essentially barren—merely pleasure or a useless desire, which produces nothing. "These delights and amorous adventures, this cheap paradise, seem at the time to be the height of passion, and what the whole world craves; time seems to stand still forever . . . , and suddenly, one sees it as a mere bagatelle." Extra-marital sex is simply deception, intimacy without love, and inexorably kills sensitivity of spirit.

On the other hand, when the sexual relationship takes place in the context designed by God, that is, in marriage, it acquires a nobility and a dignity that enhance the man and woman, because it makes them nothing less than God's cooperators and sharers in some way in his creative power by bringing new life into the world—contributing to making up the number of the elect, "those accounted worthy to attain to the resurrection from the dead."

Obviously, what leads a man and a woman to join together for life is love. But what leads them to have casual sexual intercourse is not love but desire or, at best, an emotional or sentimental state, which is a fleeting thing, as every emotion or feeling is—the kind of love described somewhere as "romantic or music-hall love." When true love is present, it is life-long—in youth and old age, in sickness and health, in good times and bad. It involves, not only self-giving, but also consciousness of the fact that one is giving oneself, and a deliberate decision to keep on giving oneself, day in, day out, whatever happens. This kind of love is not dependent on sentiment or sudden, fleeting, passionate feelings: it is something much deeper than that, something solid and stable; something much more substantial than momentary sexual arousal because it is a union of two persons sharing a project, bigger than both of them, which lasts their whole life long.

Only in this context is sexual intercourse something clean and pure: that is why, as I see it, so much emphasis was put years ago on the danger of sins of impurity.

Unless I am wrong, it was in the nineteen-forties that the idea began to be current that priests were preaching too much about sins of this kind—and that this was deformative. You would think, they used to say, that the sixth commandment was the most important or even the only commandment; they are forgetting about more serious sins, as if they were of no importance—sins of injustice, for example, or sins against charity. I must confess that I myself fell for this line for a few months, until I came to see a couple of things.

The first was that all this insistence on sins of impurity was not due to their being seen as the most serious kind of sins: it was because they were the most common, because they were easier to commit, they gave the most pleasure, and they did least damage to one's reputation because they were not committed openly (I am referring to the 'forties). There was no need, and less urgency, to preach against burning one's neighbor's crops or against murder or armed robbery, even if politically motivated. What pleasure did blaspheming or murder give? Committing murder is so embarrassing that very many people go right through life without ever doing it: they have no desire to do it, nor do they find it enjoyable.

The second thing I came to see was that the sin of impurity is, in fact, *also* a sin against justice. Adultery is wrongdoing that so obviously involves injustice and harm to the wife (or husband) and children that we need say no more. And between unmarried people: what right does anyone have to take something which does not belong to him? "A man shall leave his father and mother and be joined to his wife, and the two shall become one flesh" (Mt 19:5). His wife, not someone else's. And a woman is someone's wife when God gives her to a man in marriage—not otherwise. It is *unjust* purposely to arouse another person's sexual instinct, because it means corrupting that person, and also one might well have to answer to God for a whole series of sins deriving from that first act. It is unjust to kill a soul.

Unfortunately, nowadays, instead of being taught about chastity, people are given "sex education." I don't mind telling you that that term annoys me, and if it means what it says, its content also annoys me. In the last analysis, sex is not the only thing or the most important thing in life or in a person. And a Christian needs to be educated Christianly, not sexually. A truly Christian education will also teach a person what he needs to know about sex and its purpose according to Jesus Christ's teaching, not according to the opinion of experts.

I dare say sex education was started in order to avoid unhealthy, distorted views of sex or because ignorance of the facts of life was having a disastrous effect on people's lives—although, to be honest, I must say I am not very convinced that that was indeed the case. And I'll tell you why.

First, I have not managed to work out why so much emphasis is given to sex education when so little emphasis is given to education in morality, in basic rules of civilized behavior ("good manners," as they were once called), to education about responsibilities, about freedom and sensitivity, or about how to use our reasoning powers to do what they are designed for: to discover truth. Knowing more or knowing everything about sex does not make a person better if his will is so weak that he yields at every hand's turn; it doesn't help someone who is no longer capable of distinguishing right from wrong or who is so short on sensitivity that he does not know the meaning of refinement or respect for one's own or another's intimacy.

Moreover, obsession with sex (of whatever kind and orientation) has gone so far, what with pseudoscientific surveys and countless publications and advertisements, that one cannot but remember something the philosopher Gustave Thibon* wrote: "When I read certain writers, I get the disgusting impression that they are people who go around carrying their sexual apparatus in their hands."

* Gustave Thibon (1903–2001), French philosopher.

It is not difficult to notice—one cannot help noticing—that there are a lot of people around who make a right show of themselves. I am not simply referring to writers who need to load everything with sex, who think that fiction is dull unless it is erotic. It is really amazing to see how dirty some people's imagination is; the only thing that arouses comparable amazement is the degree to which people's sense of modesty and decorum has disappeared. I am referring to public exhibition of intimate things that should be expressed only in private (quite apart from whether they are licit or not); I am referring to that lack of consideration for others that turns cafes, cinemas, beaches, gardens, parking lots, and streets into forbidden territory for those who have not yet managed to "overcome" a certain sensitivity that makes them feel sick when they witness displays of affection (let's call them that) from couples who apparently have an uncontrollable urge to give external expression to their feelings for one another; I am referring to the attack on the freedom of others that is involved in imposing on them scenes there is no reason for them to have to see, because they have a right to public places not being turned into something else entirely.

In a pseudoscientific article on sex education, published in a Sunday supplement, I found the Nordic countries being praised as "pioneers of the demythification of sex." Seemingly, "the West," as it's called, owes them a debt. Does it really owe them anything for reducing sex to the animal level and stripping it of its human dimension? Does it owe them something for sacrificing modesty, decency, intimacy, respect, honor, and the family on the altar of the most useless and worthless act of selfishness? One author has written—and put his name to his words—that "social structures are unbelievably backward in meeting the demands of free love." Very likely.

You would need to go right back to the degenerate structures of ancient times in the heyday of their corruption to find a suitable model.

I don't know exactly what results have been achieved since "sex education" came into vogue. Not very good ones, I am afraid. Maybe headway has been made in avoiding sexual repression. By dint of treating this subject as pure biology, treating everything sexual as natural and innocent and so well-geared to people's make-up and love and the rest, some young, sexually educated people nowadays commit this kind of sin so blithely that they go to Holy Communion afterward without a thought. Obviously, they have been taught that when they do these things "for love," they don't constitute a sin: they are sinful only when they do them with an erotic intent. And who is crazy enough to act sinfully out of eroticism when he can do the same thing innocently, out of "love"? They try to show that the real evil is repression. But a dog is repressed if it performs certain innocent, natural functions on the living-room carpet; a violent child is repressed when it goes on the rampage; an idler is repressed when he tries to sponge on others; a gang member or a drug addict is brought under control. Or, at least, he should be brought under control, if one wants to train and educate him. "Is this fruit so delectable, that you eat it every day and make it as necessary as the air you breathe and sacrifice to it so many holy possibilities that lie dormant within you? No. It is stale and insipid, it turns putrid in your mouth. Yet it is the easiest kind of fruit to pick. It hangs from the lowest branch of all!" (Gustave Thibon).

Sometimes I get the impression that these "educators" are trying to destroy the young generation. They deceive you, abuse your lack of knowledge, take advantage of your inexperience. All these pseudoscientists with

their pedantic claptrap go on about "pre-marital" relations, about the need, in terms of physical health and
mental balance, that is met by sexual release every so
often, about the acceptability of masturbation, and on
and on. All this dirty reading matter is carefully designed (or diabolically designed?) and provided in carefully measured doses and authoritatively spread abroad
to corrupt men and women, who are made in the image
of God.

In this connection, the onslaught against women that
we are witnessing is quite notable. Women are designed
to be the heart of the family, the first (and most influential) educators of children; it is women who keep the
home together when everything else, perhaps, decays
little by little. The surest way, the best way, to have done
with the family is to degrade womanhood: and certainly a
lot has been done in that direction. Women's sense of
modesty has been undermined (someone told them about
"taboos," and they believed them); the most intimate relationships that can exist between man and woman have
been reduced to an animal level, to pure biology, stripped
of all their refinement and depth and mystery. And if it
has come about that womanhood is scarcely respected
at all anywhere (I am talking about so-called civilized
countries), the reason is that women, by renouncing modesty, have begun to lose their self-respect. I think that a
large part has been played in this by the whole tide of
sexual literature that goes into enormous detail, with
drawings and photographs, in popular books and luxury
editions, not only on the basics but even on peripheral
matters, which serve no purpose and which explore every
possible sexual aberration, with detailed descriptions and
even illustrations. Certainly this has achieved its object of
doing away with "inhibitions"—the kind of inhibitions
that a person used to shed only if he became inebriated.

That's the way I see it and know it to be. I do know that all these things are generally acceptable nowadays, but what the world today, the permissive society, the consumer society, or however you describe it, really thinks does not carry much weight with me. What does carry weight with me and with you, I hope, is what is good in the sight of God. And in case you haven't been taught, I feel I must put before you some things the Church has always taught as coming from Jesus Christ.

Any type of sexual relationship outside of marriage is fornication, no matter what pretext is offered for it. Husband with *his* wife, wife with *her* husband, and in the right way, in line with nature: this is lawful, good, and holy. "Do you not know that your bodies are members of Christ? Shall I therefore take the members of Christ and make them members of a prostitute? Never! Do you not know that he who joins himself to a prostitute becomes one body with her? For, as it is written, 'The two shall become one flesh.' But he who is united to the Lord becomes one spirit with him. Shun immorality. Every other sin which a man commits is outside the body; but the immoral man sins against his own body. Do you not know that your body is a temple of the Holy Spirit within you, which you have from God? You are not your own; you were bought with a price. So glorify God in your body" (1 Cor 6:15–20). That comes from Saint Paul; we are temples of God, and our body has been sanctified by baptism, which makes it the dwelling place of the Holy Spirit. The sin of impurity is a kind of profanation of something holy.

"For this is the will of God, your sanctification: that you abstain from unchastity; that each one of you know how to take a wife for himself in holiness and honor, not in the passion of lust like heathen who do not know God; that no man transgress, and wrong his brother in this matter, because the Lord is an avenger in all these things, as we solemnly forewarned you" (1 Thess 4: 3–6). I am afraid that this very clear teaching is not to be found in sex-education programs.

And, yet, these are things you need to be told. Do you know why? Because these texts—and a few others I won't quote because I don't want to go on too long— show that chastity is education—training—of one's sexual instinct. Not its *repression*, but its *education*. Believe me, I assure you the sixth commandment is not something arbitrary: as you can well appreciate, it would be an insult to God to think that he issues commands for no reason. The sixth commandment is designed to preserve the beauty, nobility, and enormous dignity of human love, to preserve it from the kind of degeneracy that results from a will deformed by original sin: from vileness, from despicable egoism, from destructive selfishness. Sexual education, therefore, in the Christian sense of the term, is the education of a person in chastity, which is not a negative virtue. It is something very positive because it is nothing less than the affirmation of the holiness of the body. The body is created by God and destined to resurrection, and therefore it too should praise its Creator. That is why Saint Augustine said, "Why do you follow your flesh? Turn around and let it follow you." Chastity is really the prayer of the body, the way our body prays.

If you think about this, it will help you see what love really is, and it will turn you away from all those other things that can usurp, and pollute, the name of love. The characteristic that acts, at least to some degree, as the test of genuine love, as what differentiates it from something masquerading as love, is respect. If you do not respect the person you say you love; if you take by force (on whatever grounds you claim) something that someone cannot, and should not, honorably give; if you destroy a person's intimacy; if you degrade and lower a person; if you ask someone to do something that offends God, then you do not love that person. What you are doing is, simply, loving yourself and using the other person for your own pleasure. Someone who acts like that does not know how to love; he knows only how to own, how to possess. And he leaves behind in his wake a landscape of ruins, something he can recall only with shame—moral wretchedness.

Shame and modesty are not the product of taboos that arose out of prudery or convention. They are natural things, not something artificial. They are the defenses nature uses to protect personal intimacy, which should not be displayed in the public street; they are signals which define limits that should not be crossed except for very serious reasons; and they act as alarm bells, warning that danger is on the horizon. We would do well to heed them.

You are young people: the welfare of the Church and, therefore, of the world looks to you. Therefore I should like to end by repeating some words from *The Way*, words that were written for you to hear: "There is need for a crusade of manliness and purity to counteract and nullify the savage work of those who think that man is a beast. And that crusade is *your* work" (no. 121). I pray our Lady to let you see this and to encourage you to take up this urgent task of moral teaching.

10

Spiritual Guidance

"How is it that you do not understand this?"

Saint John tells us in his Gospel of an important citizen of Jerusalem who went to visit Jesus. Apparently the reason for his visit was to check out this man about whom people were talking. The citizen's name was Nicodemus; he belonged to the sect of the Pharisees, and he was regarded as "a ruler of the Jews."

Saint John gives one interesting little detail about this interview: Nicodemus went to see Jesus "by night." He didn't go in the daytime; he went by night. Of course it may simply have been that Jesus was so busy preaching the good news that he had no time during the day to have a quiet conversation with such an important gentleman. But it is also possible that Nicodemus did not want to risk being seen visiting someone who was referred to, somewhat pejoratively, as "the son of the carpenter" and who was known never to have attended classes with the doctors of the law in the Temple.

As I say, the first reason is possible, but I am more inclined, instinctively, toward the second. Nicodemus had heard things about Jesus that impelled him to go to see him for himself; yet the facts at his disposal—that Jesus was the son of Mary and a carpenter from Nazareth; that he had lived for thirty years in an obscure village; that he had received no formal education and was unknown to the doctors of the law who taught in the Temple—did not say much in Jesus' favor. On the other hand, who was Amos when the Most High chose him to be his spokesman? . . . a rough, uneducated shepherd. Prudence prevailed, therefore, because an important man could not risk making himself look ridiculous—like a gullible man who will believe anything. The proud and closed world of the Pharisees tended to make men very cautious. Even toward the end of Jesus' preaching, Saint John could still note, "Nevertheless many even of the authorities believed in him, but for fear of the Pharisees they did not confess it, lest they should be put out of the synagogue" (Jn 12:42).

In any event, this really does not matter very much now. What I want to focus on today is the conversation that took place, or, rather, part of it. Nicodemus begins in a very clever and mannerly way: "Rabbi, we know that you are a teacher come from God; for no one can do these signs that you do, unless God is with him" (Jn 3:2). The way he puts it invites Jesus to agree with him and even to disclose the fact that he is the Son of God and has a mission from God. So, Nicodemus is setting the direction of the conversation. But that is as far as it goes.

Jesus replied to him, "Truly, truly, I say to you, unless one is born anew, he cannot see the kingdom of God." And then Nicodemus asks, "How can a man be born when he is old? How can a man enter a second time into his mother's womb and be born?"

The conversation has barely begun, and Nicodemus is already disconcerted: Jesus makes a simple statement, and this ruler of the Jews, this educated Pharisee, well-versed in the Scriptures, is asking questions like a small boy. Jesus explains:

> "Truly, truly, I say to you, unless one is born of water and the Spirit, he cannot enter the kingdom of God. That which is born of the flesh is flesh, and that which is born of the Spirit is spirit. Do not marvel that I said to you, 'You must be born anew.' The wind blows where it wills,

and you hear the sound of it, but you do not know whence
it comes or whither it goes; so it is with every one who is
born of the Spirit." Nicodemus said to him. "How can this
be?" Jesus answered him, "Are you a teacher of Israel, and
yet you do not understand this?" (Jn 3:5–10).

This was probably not the way Nicodemus would have
liked the conversation to go; he would have preferred it
to follow the line of his own opening remarks. Was Jesus,
or was he not, a teacher sent by God? Or was he something more than just a teacher? What were his plans?
What was his attitude toward the Sanhedrin and to its
two main groupings, the Pharisees and the Sadducees?
Nicodemus needed to know this; he wanted to be sure
where he stood. And here was Jesus going off in another
direction entirely, somewhere quite unexpected. He was
speaking to him about a world in which Nicodemus was
a total stranger, a world in which he was lost, like a child
in a big city. What was happening? For he, Nicodemus,
was not an ignorant man; he was a respected person, a
teacher of the law, someone who knew the Scriptures,
and a man of experience.

The only problem was that this was not enough. Despite his age, his prestige, his education, and his experience, as far as things to do with the Kingdom of heaven
were concerned, Nicodemus was, really, a child who
needed to be guided by someone who knew what was
what. Jesus showed him this quite clearly: he told him
that, so far as the Kingdom of God was concerned, he
had no notion where he was going.

There is nothing surprising about this; Jesus is not in
any way humiliating Nicodemus. If you have not learned
something, then you don't know anything about it. And
how could Nicodemus know about the mysteries of the
world of grace, which Jesus was, at that very period,
beginning to reveal to people by means of step-by-step

teaching? If anyone of us stops to think, he will realize from his own experience that we are ignorant about things until we learn about them.

I suppose that is why there are such things as schools, institutes, and universities, why new centers of education and training are continually being set up, and why the state tries to insure that its citizens are literate and have access to as much education as they can take. We refer to people "learning a trade"; there is nothing embarrassing about being a learner. I have yet to find anyone who is ashamed to take direction from a supervisor when he is doing a thesis; no one accepts this kind of guidance on sufferance, just because those are the regulations. These regulations exist because a person doing a thesis needs someone who can guide him in a direction where he has never gone before.

Of course, I am referring to the normal situation, because there are cases where direction is given in name only. But anyone who has found himself in that situation (except perhaps a genius, and there are not many geniuses around) knows full well that he wasted a lot of time, did a lot of useless work, made a lot of mistakes, and in the end came out worse than he would have if his supervisor had bothered to mark his card at the right time.

All this is common sense, and you should have no difficulty in seeing it. Well then, when we come to the most important question of all, the one to do with personal salvation, which is a matter of life and death, it would appear that none of this holds good, that one can get by without even a minimum amount of reasoning. Common sense is tossed into a corner, and people smother even their ability to think straight; logic and straight thinking are not given a look in. What is quite inadmissible in any field of learning, any kind of business or trade, any activity at all, is made almost the norm when it comes to the Kingdom of God, the life of grace—an area, besides, that is absolutely basic for any Christian.

I am not talking about theories but about facts. Nowadays it is quite common for people to consult doctors, not only in cases of urgent need, but periodically, to get a check-up to make sure everything is all right: "preventive medicine" it is called. Here we are talking of the health of the body, and, obviously, prevention is better than cure. But apparently the soul is not regarded as having the same importance, judging from the casual way we treat it.

Yet the soul is very important. It is so important that the fate of the body depends on it: "Do not fear those who kill the body, and after that have no more that they can do. But I will warn you whom to fear: fear him who, after he has killed, has power to cast into hell" (Lk 12:4–5). There is a resurrection of the body, which means that if we save our soul we have also saved our body; but we will have ruined it forever if, by earning condemnation, we draw down eternal death upon it.

If you do not learn about something, you don't know it. Apart from the basic catechism you learn for First Holy Communion; apart from what a person remembers a little vaguely, because he has not yet managed to forget it, from classes and devotions during his school years; what do most adults know about the supernatural life, that life which a person should be living because he is a Christian?

Very little, it seems to me. And today, as far as young people are concerned, to judge from my experience, even less. It is still possible to meet mature adults who, in spite of their neglect of things to do with God and their own soul, still have a good grasp of basic ideas, basic truths, which they learned from the catechism. But I am afraid that in recent years even this basic education has been missing. On the one hand, some catechisms (I don't mind calling them "graded religious textbooks") do not seem to be absolutely reliable as far as doctrinal content goes, or as complete as they ought to be, that is, they do not cover everything they should cover, all the basics. On the other hand, teachers are not keen on children learning things by heart; they want the children to reason things out and extend their horizon to include human problems (underdevelopment, social justice, and so on) to insure that they have a good grounding in charity, the central virtue for a Christian. The net effect of this policy is that children are, to some extent, vague and fuzzy about ideas, and within a few years they are incapable of distinguishing what is essential from what is accessory. When they reach university age, they are usually disorientated and empty-headed as far as religion is concerned. They seldom know by heart those simple, clear answers about the key truths of faith. On the other hand, they do have a notion about and can discuss fairly ably socioeconomic questions tinged with a vague religious coloring: and they believe in these things. They also think that all this has to do with a renewal of the Christian life and is the very essence of the Gospel—those students, that is, who still take a certain interest in their faith.

I am referring, as I suppose you can see, to spiritual guidance, spiritual direction, and I am perfectly well aware that this is a very unpopular subject these days. Well, I should like to point out that popularity is a value not worth bothering about. A singer will do everything he can to be popular; and he is right to do so, because that is his aim: if he is not popular he is nothing. An advertising agent will rack his brains to find a slogan to make a deodorant popular: that's how he earns his living. But if a priest wants to be popular, then it is better if he spends his time at something else, because it is not his job to please people; his job is to please God. It is not for him to be "aware" of the direction in which the world is being drawn; what he has to be aware of is revealed truth; he is not called to be faithful to his time; he is called to be faithful to Christ. And although there is a tendency today to imitate that general who, presiding over a shameful retreat of his men, races ahead of them toward the rear guard and tells the shocked civilians, to justify himself, "What do you expect? A general must always be at the head of his troops!" I doubt very much if he is doing the right thing. Jesus was not out to make himself popular; he did not tailor his message to suit people. He had come to say what he had heard from the Father, and that was what he did. And you know what it cost him to do that.

Let's not look back over history. Today it is not easy to find among Christians, in general, even an interest in learning basic ideas about the supernatural life; few people look for guidance about spiritual things, things to do with their own soul. A sociological survey, of the kind that is so much in vogue, would probably find that spiritual guidance is "old-fashioned," and probably it would not make clear whether it was the term that is old-fashioned, its content, or both. Surveys would probably also show that the clientele of psychiatrists, psychologists, marriage counselors, and experts had grown in the same proportion as confession and spiritual guidance had decreased.

So, I will speak to you about spiritual direction, and I shall begin by asking you to bear in mind the case of Nicodemus: he was an educated man, experienced, well versed in the Scriptures, a teacher of the law, and yet he

needed someone to give him guidance about the supernatural life of grace. Am I going too far if I assert that all
of you need someone to guide you on the road to salvation if you are not to remain spiritual dwarfs or, what's
worse, go off course entirely?

I don't think I'm wrong if I say that on the subject of
man's road to God (that is, his road to total fulfillment)
no one, in the normal course of events, is self-sufficient.
No one can give himself (or others) what he does not
have; and ignorance is corrected by reading, reflection,
and study. But even there guidance is called for, because
not every book is useful, and some books are clearly and
openly erroneous. There are also, and perhaps more in
this field than in others, plenty of books dealing with
God, Jesus Christ, and the Church that are written by
incompetent authors.

When I say "incompetent," I am not referring to their
lack of talent but to their lack of competence. A person is
competent when he *knows* the subject in question. And
because we are referring to certain truths that the
Church possesses and has been teaching unchanged for
twenty centuries, only he who has learned these truths
and retains them *faithfully* is competent to teach them to
others. It is not a matter of talent (although that can
influence, very much so, the *way* one conveys these
truths); at least, it is not only a matter of truth but, above
all, of fidelity, because it is not a question of creating or
inventing something but of passing it on to others. The
teaching that has to do with salvation is not something
that one invents: this is obvious. I see no reason why
great talent is necessarily exempt from the risk of saying
stupid things if the speaker is dealing with something of
which he is ignorant (I could even give you a few examples); and to deal with the doctrine about salvation,
Christ, the soul, the Church, the supernatural life, the

way God works in the soul, it is not enough for someone to have talent or even to have a Nobel prize in physics, medicine, literature, or biology. What one needs is to know the doctrine and to know it well. That is what comes first.

But a number of other things are necessary, including, I would dare to say, a certain practice, a certain experience. A spiritual director is not a theorist who provides an intellectual solution to problems posed to him. It is not only that he has to have learned a pile of good books, although he does need that (you are aware that Saint Teresa of Avila insisted that spiritual directors should be "well read); he himself needs to have an interior life; he needs to be striving to grow in wisdom and grace, and in faith, hope, and charity; and he himself needs to be receiving spiritual guidance. For a very simple reason: the Gospel is not a philosophical system; it is life. If a person is not striving to live that life, he cannot understand what it is about, in all its breadth and depth; and no one can guide another unless he knows the way. Well, "the wind blows where it wills, and you hear the sound of it, but you do not know whence it comes or whither it goes" (Jn 3:8). Do you see? One does not know, and therefore one needs someone *other than oneself,* someone who, in addition to having knowledge and experience, possesses the necessary light, which God communicates by means of that gift which is known as "grace of state" (a special help to carry out a God-given task); someone who can discern what comes from God and what does not because it comes from one's own spirit or from the devil; someone who guides us through a network of roads, along the one road that leads to eternal life.

Even a doctor, no matter how eminent he may be, puts himself in the hands of other doctors when he is ill—he cannot be both subject and object of his own observation, save at the risk of making a fatal error. And a doctor knows what's what. Well, in things to do with the interior life (which is not a closed, independent world of its own, because no individual is a collection of separate compartments), not even a good theologian (not to mention bad theologians), not even a bishop, not even the Pope himself can afford the luxury of doing without the human and supernatural help that God provides through the priest. Of course this help can be rejected, and a person can let himself be guided by his own spirit; of course, he must also then accept the consequences, none of which is likely to be very healthy.

As far as you are concerned, I do not know why you are allergic to letting yourselves be given direction concerning the things of God, which are of concern to your own present and future happiness. I can't believe that it is due to "alienation," unless that is just an excuse, which you yourselves can see through or which you have accepted without even spending a few minutes studying to see if it makes sense. What I mean is that if you think about it a bit you will have to agree that, in that case, children should not be sent to school because that would involve alienation, or people should not be allowed to fall in love, for the same reason. And if you think a bit more you will see that, on your hypothesis, education, training, and guidance lead inevitably to alienation: the world is full of alienated people who alienate themselves in all sorts of things. Sociologists (and some clerics) alienate themselves in sociology; those who do not believe in confession alienate themselves in psychiatry; almost everyone (today, at least) alienates himself in the economy; Marxists do it in Marx, and so on: everyone, even the scientist, is alienating himself. However, in actual fact, the only people really alienated are credulous people (not men of faith), that is, those who believe in theories instead of believing in truths.

But spiritual direction, of all things, does not aim at turning the person who wants to receive it into an unthinking robot that does only what other people tell him to do. Spiritual direction does not take away a person's freedom or freeze his ability to think for himself because it does not impose anything; what it does is teach the ways of grace and the operations of the Holy Spirit in souls. Spiritual direction helps the person who is being guided to develop the criteria that will enable him to act as a true disciple of Christ—that is, as a Christian—in whatever situation he finds himself.

I think it is true that young people (I am speaking in general)—as well as very many mature people—reject the teaching authority of the Church and do not accept any criteria that they have not devised on their own. And you can see the results. It is then, as a last resort, that they have recourse to others (usually a priest) to solve the problem or the situation created by their ignorance (or their petulance?), which sometimes has even done damage to lives other than their own. And sometimes, when this stage is reached, there are those who complain because they are not given a panacea that works instantly and in line with their desires and solves their problem or situation, leaving things just the way they were originally.

There are some things you cannot play around with. I mean, you can if you want to, but you must take the consequences. What one does or does not do is never something entirely personal: we live amid other people, people with whom we are connected, and everything we do can affect them for better or worse, helping or hindering. And if one does not have standards based on the Truth, then one can do irreparable damage.

Naturally, I would like to have been so convincing that on reading this you decide to look for spiritual direction for yourself. In case God does inspire you to do just that, I should like to give you one last piece of advice.

Make a careful search to find a suitable person to whom to entrust your soul. There are many wolves in sheep's clothing doing the rounds these days. If you fall into their hands, you could be destroyed, although if you have the right intention I am sure that God will find a way to prevent any irreparable damage being done. So, you can see that even in this matter of choosing a guide you need to have the right criterion. And this criterion can be taken from observing the doctrine and the lifestyle of the person you are thinking of choosing as a spiritual guide. You should observe even his appearance: you may think I am being silly, but I am not. At least I'm not being totally silly, because you can tell a lot from the outside about the inside. Although I think that on this point you have—I hope I'm not wrong—a kind of instinct that will keep you safe, you should still take a few precautions, and the first is that of changing your director the moment you see that instead of having a supernatural concern for your soul his interest seems to turn on subjects of religious sociology or current affairs; when, instead of instilling peace in your soul, he leaves you disturbed; when, instead of letting you see what Jesus Christ demands of one who believes and trusts in him, he is too inclined to accommodate your comfort or your laziness or he scarcely gives any importance to prayer, mortification, and the sacraments.

To sum up: in the same way as when you want to be a doctor you put yourselves under the instructions of people who know and practice medicine in order to learn from them things you do not know; just as you need a guide to lead you in difficult terrain, unmapped territory where there are no roads, or too many roads; you have the same need for someone to guide you on your way to God. Nicodemus was well versed in the Scriptures, he was a man of experience and a doctor of the law. *You* are not very familiar with the Scriptures, you do not have experience of divine things (nor, I suggest, of human things), you do not know theology. And if Nicodemus was a child in the things of the spirit and of the Kingdom of God and if he needed a guide to show him the way, as Jesus clearly proved to him, can you tell me, in heaven's name, what grounds you have for thinking that you can do without something every mortal man, even one with common sense, needs?

11

Commitment to Christ

"He who acknowledges me before men . . ."

In chapter ten of his Gospel, Saint Matthew gathers together some of the instructions Jesus had probably given his disciples at different times. As you may know, Saint Matthew does not follow a chronological order in his narrative. He follows what today we call a thematic order, gathering together various interconnected teachings, which were given originally on different occasions.

Among the teachings of Jesus in this chapter, we find one in which he warns his disciples about what lies in store for them because of their fidelity to the Gospel: "You will be hated by all for my name's sake." He foretold what they would have to suffer because of him: they would be persecuted, denounced, brought before judges, and flogged; he encouraged them not to fear those who can kill only the body, because in actual fact they cannot really do much harm; he warned them to fear him who can kill both body and soul, casting them into hell. He instilled confidence in them, making them see that if God's concern was so great that not a sparrow could fall to the ground without his permission, then how much more would he care for them, who were of more value than many sparrows. And he concluded with these words: "Every one who acknowledges me before men, I also will acknowledge before my Father who is in heaven; but whoever denies me before men, I also will deny before my Father who is in heaven" (Mt 10: 32–34).

This seems fairly just, at least insofar as we men understand justice. If a person acknowledges Jesus before men, gives proof of his loyalty and fidelity, of his commitment to Christ in the midst of difficulties, at the loss, perhaps, of earthly goods, physical integrity, and even life, then it seems logical that as a reward and compensation Jesus should acknowledge him before his heavenly Father. He has told us that, at the end of the hunt, the standard we use in judging will be the standard by which we ourselves are judged. By acknowledging or denying him we are determining the measure with which he is going to evaluate our attitude toward him.

At the same time it is clear that when Jesus was instructing his disciples about what those who believe in him would have to suffer for his name's sake, he did not mean to imply that *all* his disciples would have to pass through those trials nor that they would *always* have to live under such threats. What does seem clear is that by being his disciples they should be ready for anything and everything, rather than deny him. If you read the Gospel carefully, you will find that Jesus' teaching in this regard is demanding: anyone who loves father or mother or children or life more than him cannot be his disciple. He cannot be a disciple because, when forced to choose between Jesus Christ—who is God and man—and other men, he would not choose Christ. This makes it impossible for him to be a disciple and follower of the Master.

Undoubtedly, not all times and circumstances are the same, but the need to acknowledge Jesus publicly and explicitly, not only in word but also in deed, becomes obligatory in particular situations, at those moments when not to acknowledge him would be the equivalent of denying him.

Twenty-five or fifty years ago,* and perhaps even less,

* This essay was first published in 1973.

132

I don't think there was any great problem in this regard in Western Europe. There were in the Church a certain number of Catholics who lived far from God without going to the extreme of denying their faith. "Non-practicing" Catholics we called them. In general, their problems had more to do with morals than doctrine, and in many cases they were simply the result of ignorance. Most of them welcomed the opportunity to receive the sacraments when the moment of truth came, and they were reconciled with God.

There was another small minority of Christians who sincerely struggled to grow in grace, who had interior life and tried to live in conformity with their faith. I don't say they were perfect, or even attractive, but at least they tried honestly to please God.

And then there was the majority. Certainly not cut off from God, but not too close to him either. Neither hot not cold, they lived in a comfortable temperate climate, more or less halfway between the Arctic and the Equator. Comfortably settled in the Church, they ran the risk of neither condemnation nor holiness; they were without great sins but without great virtues either. Generally they kept the commandments of the Church, and not so generally the commandments of God. They had little or no sense of responsibility as members of the mystical Body of Christ, being convinced that the Church was there more to serve them than they to serve her. In the Barque of Peter they enjoyed the privileges of passengers but carefully shunned the inconveniences that lay on the crew—the effort, the responsibility, being on watch, the toil and slogging involved in running a ship. This large group was noted for its mediocrity.

In such a broad cross section of Church members, there were all sorts—from the calculators, who weighed up the advantages and disadvantages and wished to purchase their salvation at the lowest price; to people who knew how to swim and still keep their clothing on; to people who tried to show that, yes, indeed, it was possible to serve two masters; and, finally, to those who tried again and again to free themselves from a state of habitual sin or lukewarmness and grow in love of God. More than calculators, it seems to me that the vast majority were merely negligent, weak, or apathetic, distracted by things more immediately to hand, taken in by what was pleasant and easy. With regard to the Kingdom of heaven they were like those who, in this life, are anemic, lame, blind, or deaf and mute. They all survived, even the calculators, not by their own efforts but because they were kept afloat. There were structures (customs, discipline, environment, authority, rules, and regulations) around them that protected them and supported them in their weakness. Thanks to these structures, and in spite of their listlessness, they were able to stay afloat. They existed in a hothouse, but they didn't *live*.

However, to do that today is all but impossible. In these last years, many structures have come down, and they have not been replaced by anything to shore up our weakness. There is no support for the weak, no protection for the flabby, no scaffolding for the apathetic. No discipline, no authority, no law, no rules and regulations, no good customs and environment to keep them from falling.

The results are to be seen. As soon as these supports were removed, as soon as guiding principles were undermined, many fell, losing the meager supernatural life they once had and, in some cases, also their good morals and even their faith. Others, without any change on the outside, fell so low on the inside that it is merely a question of time until, like dead members, they abandon the living Body, unless a miracle of grace revives them.

The atmosphere is so replete with errors and untruths contrary to the teaching of Christ that a great number of those who formerly lived in the hothouse now wander along without knowing what exactly they ought to believe or what is good and what is bad, what God commands and what he forbids.

A purification of the Church? If by purification is meant the dumping of ballast—those Catholics who were limping along, sickly, almost lifeless, and making no contribution—then the operation has been a success, because those Catholics have been left on the pier. They have not come through; they have sunk like stones. They were told they were adults, but no one stopped to make sure that they had the strength and maturity of adulthood. They hadn't.

As far as I can see, you young people are in a difficult situation. You don't have around you Christian structures that you can grab onto while you grow in interior life until such time as you can make do for yourselves. The situation of a Christian in the world has always been like that of a swimmer in the middle of a powerful river; he either swims strongly and energetically upstream against the current or he is swept along by it until he is lost in the ocean. The nets that were strung out here and there, from one bank to the other, nets fashioned by centuries of Christian experience, as a help to the weary swimmers who needed a breather, or at least a chance to hold on a while and not be swept away, are no longer in place. Those nets served to give a bit of encouragement to weakened souls or, at least, they were supposed to. Now that they have been torn down and destroyed, there is nothing left to protect us from our own weakness.

In other words, times have changed. Today it is ever more difficult to remain in no-man's-land, in a comfortable state of mediocrity, neither cold nor hot. And yet there is an urgent need for us to take a stand, to define ourselves, not with our mouths, but integrally, by the way we live—either for him or against him, making our choice and accepting the consequences.

Twenty-five years ago, there was hardly any need for the virtue of fortitude if one wanted to continue as a member of the Church. The faith of the ordinary Catholic was in no way threatened or, at the very least, one reacted at the first sign of danger. The Magisterium was accepted by all, starting with us priests. I am sure you have all heard the witticism that exclaimed: "Surely you are not going to risk damnation for a point of dogma, are you?" That gives some idea of the way things were.

It was due, no doubt, to the steps that were taken to protect people's faith. Our pastors saw to it that error was not mixed in with good doctrine. If opinions or statements of philosophers or theologians that were contrary to the faith, to the truths revealed by God, began to do the rounds, they were identified and condemned. And if the theologian or philosopher did not humbly accept the judgment of the Church, if he persisted in teaching what the Magisterium declared to be opposed to Catholic faith, then evidently he did not believe everything that the Church believes and professes, and, therefore, he cut himself off from the Church. At times the Church made a public declaration to that effect, and the result was that such erroneous teachings could do little to harm the faith of Catholics. The faithful knew that these teachings were wrong and that those who upheld them were by that very fact excluded from the Mystical Body of Christ. If I remember correctly, it was generally held at that time, and even up to recently, that there was nothing worse than being separated from the Church, being outside the communion of the faithful and deprived of the sacraments. That thought alone was enough to freeze one's soul. So, the danger to Catholics from false teaching was a remote one indeed.

But today it is not. As I have already said, times have changed. Things are not as they used to be when the faith was generally adhered to without much bother. Nor are things like they once were in the times before Constantine—at least not in the Western world—when Christians were in danger of persecution, calumny, and denunciation, were looked upon as enemies destined for extinction, and had to live heroically in a hostile environment. So hostile was it that one had to be always ready to confess one's faith publicly and, by doing so, perhaps to lose one's life. The only other alternative was apostasy. There was no room for playacting and mental reservations, going through the motions of worshipping idols and only pretending to do so. It wasn't enough to believe, and to believe firmly; one had to *confess one's faith*. Not to act thus was the equivalent of apostatizing, denying Jesus Christ.

The times in which we live are different. Our faith is not protected as it was up to recently; now it is threatened and must be held on to with a struggle. Not that it is threatened by physical violence from outside, as in the first centuries. In fact, that kind of threat is not very useful, and I'm sure the devil knows it; he will have learned by experience. The persecutions of pagan Rome, and the physically violent ones of our own day, in Communist dominated countries, for example, do not make apostates but martyrs, saints, and confessors, witnesses to the divine nature of Catholic faith. Today the danger that assails the faithful is more subtle and more effective. First, because it does not employ violence or brute force and so it does not put people on guard or provoke them into a healthy reaction or heroic resistance. Second, because the danger comes not from outside the Church but from within. Pope Paul VI was very explicit when he spoke of the cracks through which the smoke of Satan had entered the Church, thinning its air, spreading a mist that prevented things being seen clearly, erasing boundary lines, and throwing objects into the shadows. He also spoke very clearly of the devil, a liar and the father of lies, a pervert who wants to pervert others, a murderer from the beginning. In the short term, this diabolical activity in the Church tends less to provoke public apostasies than to lead to a gradual abandonment of faith in Christ and to the emplacement of faith in some idol, preferably man himself. There is abandonment, not by formal denial, but by substitution, watering down, or subterfuge. No formal apostasy but a de facto one.

I wonder if any of you is acquainted with the Athanasian Creed. It is a very old, very clear, precise profession of faith, whose opening and closing words have always struck me forcibly. It starts like this: "Whoever wishes to be saved must, above all, keep the Catholic faith; for unless a person keeps this faith whole and entire, he will undoubtedly be lost forever." It ends with the following warning: "This is the Catholic faith. Everyone must believe it, firmly and steadfastly; otherwise he cannot be saved." One has to profess the Catholic faith *wholly and entirely, steadfastly and firmly.* If one doesn't believe all that the Church believes and teaches, if one believes not steadfastly but only intermittently, if one is not faithful to the content of the faith and to all its consequences, if one violates the faith in any way, then beware, because one is in danger of making shipwreck of one's faith and of being excluded (at least de facto) from communion with the Church.

As far as I can see, there are many such cases in the world today. Now, it is not for me to pass judgment on what is going on, much less to judge others, but we do need to reflect. A Catholic who defends divorce and thereby affirms that marriage is not indissoluble evidently does not profess the faith of the Church, which teaches, in line with the Gospel, that marriage is indissoluble because "what God has joined together let no man put asunder." Can we say that in such a case the Catholic faith is professed *wholly*? Can a priest or a doctor who recommends the use of contraceptives because, in his opinion, a family is large enough, or the health of the woman makes it dangerous to have another pregnancy, or the family is not well off, or there are already too many people in the world: can he be said to be in communion with the Pope, who openly, clearly, publicly, and expressly has affirmed the illicit nature of such means? Can a person be said to profess *all* that the Church teaches if he doesn't accept the teaching of the Magisterium even when it is stated so unambiguously? Isn't a psychologist, or a writer or anybody else for that matter, who publicly states that premarriage sexual relations are good and licit and opportune, simply saying that God himself has made an arbitrary decision in forbidding fornication and that the Church is wrong in teaching what cannot and ought not be done in virtue of the divine command? Is such a person professing the Catholic faith in its entirety?

Can a Catholic be a Marxist? Yes, provided he ceases to be a Catholic. On this point, too, the Church is very explicit and has been officially so since 1949. At that time, the question was asked: Do Catholics who profess the materialist and anti-Christian teaching of Marxism, and those who spread such teaching, incur, *ipso facto*, excommunication reserved to the Holy See? The answer was: Yes, they do. A Catholic who becomes a Marxist is an apostate from the faith; he does not follow Christ, he does not even believe in Christ. He believes in and follows Marx. He does not believe in God our Creator but in the kind of thing Marx called matter. He does not believe in Jesus Christ our Savior (in the USSR the Communist Party denied for years that he had even existed). He does not believe in a future life, in heaven or hell, but he does believe in the earthly paradise of a classless society. He believes, with Marx, that the Church of Christ is part of the superstructure, the opium of the people and the instrument of capitalism, and he works to destroy her. You can tell me whether such a person can still be called a Christian.

I was saying a while back that, in matters to do with faith, the situation of young people is difficult. It is so, above all, because of the rarification and contamination of the Christian atmosphere. Where, in times gone by, the faithful could be almost absolutely certain that in preaching and in catechesis they would never hear anything remotely near a disagreement with the Magisterium of the Church, the same does not hold true today. It is public and notorious that even in Sunday homilies not only are the faithful given human doctrines that have nothing to do with revelation, but also erroneous opinions, often in open conflict with Catholic faith, are pressed upon them. Pope Paul VI, in the past, and now Pope John Paul II, never tired of denouncing errors regarding the blessed Eucharist, matrimony, and baptism. There is hardly a point of doctrine taught by the Church over the past twenty centuries which is not now called in question, from *within* the Church. The Creed of Paul VI (so solemnly proclaimed [June 30, 1968] during the Holy Year of Faith) and the continuing catechesis of John Paul II have not prevented the preaching, writing, and dissemination of doubts, problems, confrontations, uncertainties, insinuations, and crass errors. And it is all done so cleverly and so effectively, with such disdain for authority and discipline that, in the words of Paul VI, one has to believe that "something preternatural has come into the world to cause upset." We can all see with our own eyes what the Pope is referring to—"confusion and uneasiness in consciences, religious impoverishment, woeful defections among those living a consecrated life and those joined in faithful and indissoluble marriage."

And, we might add, a notable decrease in vocations to the priesthood, the abandonment of moral norms in favor of individual selfishness, attempts to change the Church's teaching to justify de facto situations, and so on. When clearly erroneous catechisms are published against the will of the Holy See, I wonder how one can be sure of anything, even something said by a priest. Thus it seems to me that you need to be specially fortified in your Christian faith if you wish to acknowledge Christ before men.

In these times, we need confessors of the faith, witnesses to the divine nature of revelation; but not with the same kind of valor that Christians needed in times of persecution. A different kind of fortitude is now required. Don't think that when I speak of confessing the faith, of acknowledging Jesus Christ, I am referring to loudmouths who are continually calling attention to their Catholicism by appealing to encyclicals and by alluding, at the slightest opportunity, to what the Holy Father has said in his latest address. Besides being tiresome, this kind of witnessing (if we can call it that) is not usually very effective, because those who do it seem to be forever lecturing others, reminding them gently (or so they think) of truths and norms that ought to make an impact on their lives. Of course, they don't put themselves forward as models, but, at times, they cannot hide their quiet satisfaction as they contemplate the good example they are giving. There are people like that; undoubtedly they are doing their best and have merit in the eyes of God; but that is not the kind of witnessing to which I am referring. Let me put it this way: today, and more and more as time goes on, a member of the Church who is passive is in grave danger. To overcome that danger a number of steps need to be taken.

First, there is a need for purity of doctrine. We must know well what Christ has revealed in matters of faith and morals; in morals as well, because Christianity is never a simple matter of knowing, but of living. Faith without good works is dead. "You believe that God is one; you do well. Even the demons believe—and shudder" (Jas 2: 19). Since only a person who knows the truth can detect error, by the simple method of seeing that it contradicts what he knows to be true, my advice is that you learn from a good catechism, one sufficiently broad and, at the same time, profound.

Second, life. Interior life is needed if God's grace is to fill us and be the driving force of all our actions. Imagine for a moment a hermetically sealed tank containing a gas whose atmospheric pressure is 990 millibars; this tank is surrounded by another gaseous mass whose pressure is 1030 millibars. If an opening is made in the hermetically sealed tank and the two gases are allowed to mix, the one on the outside, which is at a higher pressure, flows in, changes, and displaces the gas that was in the tank. But if the pressure of the gas in the tank is greater than that around the tank, then, when the two gases meet, it is the gas in the tank that changes the environment around it, influencing it, and displacing and substituting it.

Likewise, if the interior pressure of your soul, of your interior life, is stronger than the atmosphere around you, then you (or rather God's grace through you) will influence and change the environment. If, on the other hand, your interior pressure is low, then the world will seep in, you will be influenced, and you will conform. And if that happens, how will you bear witness to Christ if what is within you is not the teachings of Christ but the norms of society? And let me now add that your interior pressure will be low unless you are prayerful souls. I mean mental prayer, each day, at a fixed time. If you have no deep friendship with Christ, if you do not communicate with him each day, if you do not open your soul to his influence, I don't know how you can come to know and love him. Without close contact with him in prayer and in the blessed Eucharist, what personal friendship can there be between him and us? At zero interior pressure—and that comes about when we are far from Christ—we will be swept along by the spirit of this world.

And third, valor. In today's world, valor demands that we live the virtue of fortitude; we need to be strong in the faith. And this means putting to one side any and every statement, opinion, proposition, or theory not in accord with received Catholic faith, because you can be absolutely certain that assertions which contradict the truths of faith are false. I think it was Chesterton who said that all the "scientific" arguments used by the free-thinkers at the end of the last century have turned out to be false, as shown by science itself. Today we give too much authority to physics, biology, sociology, and even literature in the field of revelation. A Greek apologist of the middle of the second century told us: "No man has seen or known God, but he to whom God has revealed himself. He manifests himself through faith, the only way in which we can see him." The way God shows himself, the way to God, is the way of faith. Faith, not physics or biology or sociology or theater or essays or novels.

Given the prevailing winds in today's world, winds that lead to adoration of the world itself, you clearly can see that much valor is needed to be faithful to Christ in spite of the pressure of the environment; much valor to be faithful, as was Saint Peter of Alcantara, who put it this way in a letter to Saint Teresa of Avila: "As regards myself, I trust more the word of God than I do my own experience." Obviously, it is not the method to use in chemical research, but it is in theological research. He knew that God would never deceive him, and he also knew that his own experience might.

In any case, it is good not to lose sight of these other words of Christ, because if you reflect upon them you may learn why all these things are happening: "How can you believe, who receive glory from one another and do not seek the glory that comes from the only God?" (Jn 5:44).

12

Devotion to Mary

Pray for us.

I want to deal now with a subject that certainly doesn't absorb the attention of the average university student. It has to do with our Lady: it is the Rosary. I dare say you will think I am crazy, but I am going to try to convince you that this devotion is not only not something silly or a sign of religious immaturity or something left over from the superstitions of times gone by, but quite the contrary: it is an ingredient and, indeed, a fairly important ingredient in what ought to be the daily diet of every Christian's soul.

In fact, I would go further. I would go as far as to say that the Rosary is the thread—fine but very strong—that in these difficult times can secure those who are wavering, who are in doubt, who are weak, confused, or scandalized. Indeed, I will also tell you that it can even be the way home for those who have more or less gone away, under the spell of what they think is a great discovery, to follow those intellectual idols which, when ably manipulated, captivate young men and women just as marionettes do children. I would even say, were I not afraid you would think I was going too far, that the Rosary is also a means of making a terrifically effective contribution to changing the world.

You do understand that to talk about the Rosary in this way and to *university students* may seem a little daring. And yet I think it is worth running that risk. It must be useful to some people to hear serious and respectful

treatment of this subject, because nowadays it is the
fashion to treat the Rosary as expressive of spiritual
underdevelopment or immaturity. The trouble is that I
don't know if I can demonstrate something that to me
seems clear as crystal; so I would ask you to be a little
patient: I'll try.

Many years ago, a famous Argentinean novelist said
that one of the advance signs of a Christian's giving up
the faith was his lack of regard for devotion to our Lady.
Of course, that novelist was no theologian, but he was
very observant. He wasn't trying to make up a theory
but simply to underline something that, at least where he
was, was almost a scientific fact. And yet, what he said
had a deeper theological root than you might expect in a
casual phrase in a now forgotten novel. A mariologist
might be able to prove this to you using arguments well-
based on Scripture; but I'm afraid that that sort of thing
won't be much use to you. My feeling is that university
students nowadays are not exactly characterized by their
rigorous logic (I may be wrong). However, it may be
safer to adopt another approach; so I will use a piece
from the French writer Charles Péguy* as a starter. He
said:

> Our Lady has saved me from despair. That was my great-
> est danger. People like us have faith enough and charity
> enough: it's hope we may be short of. I emerged from this
> situation when I was writing my *Porche*. Imagine: for
> eight months I couldn't even say the Our Father.... I
> could not say, "Thy will be done." Do you realize what
> this means? I could not pray to God, because I could not
> accept his will. It is awful. It is not a matter of mouthing
> prayers. It is a matter of saying, of meaning exactly
> what you are saying. And I could not truly say "Thy will

* Charles Péguy (1873–1914) was a French Catholic poet; he was killed
during World War I.

be done." Then I prayed to Mary. Prayers addressed to Mary are "reserve" prayers. . . . There isn't one in all the liturgy, not even one, which the most miserable of sinners cannot *truly* say. In the machinery of salvation the Hail Mary is the last source of aid. You cannot be lost if you have it.

Péguy felt quite incapable of honestly praying the Our Father because he could not bring himself to say "Thy will be done." He wasn't able to submit his will to God's; he could not accept God's plan for him. A kind of evil interior rebellion prevented him. Yet what he could do was turn to our Lady—and that was precisely what he did. He could not say to God, "Thy will be done." But he could say to Mary, "Pray for us sinners, now and at the hour of our death," and, at the end of eighteen months, what had been impossible stopped being so, thanks to her whom the Church calls our Hope.

You must, of course, understand that it is a matter of being very honest, of playing clean. It is not just rolling off some formulas; no, we are very concerned to see whether what we are saying is or is not related to our interior attitude. Serious things have to be taken seriously; we have to go through the pain of a seemingly insoluble interior conflict to be able to express the problem with as much precision as Péguy could. He grasped, almost scientifically, how our Lady had saved him from despair.

For despair is the fruit of pride, its most rotten fruit. As Merton put it, despair is the corrupt luxury of preferring to be condemned rather than owe salvation to anyone distinct from one's self. There is always something in the core of each person that can give rise to an attitude of rebellion, of annoyance, or of opposition to God. This interior attitude of rebellion is generally let loose by something we have to bear and yet do not understand, something that seems an arbitrary imposition or an

injustice for which we cannot find a satisfactory explanation. Why does God allow this or that? Why has it to be
this way and not that? Why? Why? For example, sometimes attitudes of anger or opposition arise in us, due to
the suffering of innocent people or pain or hunger or all
kinds of things. . . . I refer to people who, like Péguy, are
playing clean—not to those who accuse God in order to
excuse themselves or those who rebel against God out
of pure resentment because he has not made things, not
made the world, as they would have liked it to be.

I think that in situations like this a person tends to
forget that his understanding is limited; he forgets how
much he needs to know even to glimpse a possible way
out. And yet we ought never, strictly speaking, condemn
what we do not understand or label as injustice anything
that does not fit in with our personal meaning of justice.

So, even in those cases in which one perceives (because
one has not been turned into a thing or a fanatic) an
interior hardening, which makes one, as it were, oppose
God, rebelling against his will (be it his positive or his
permissive will), even in those cases there is room for
hope, there is still someone to go to for help. Mary is
always the solution even when everything, including
hope, seems to have been lost.

It has been said of our Lady that she is "God's tenderness toward men." It is not perhaps a very theological
definition; yet I think it is as expressive and exact. You
will see why.

In all of us there is an almost inescapable tendency to
see God through ourselves. He made us in his image and
likeness, but we tend to want to make God in our image
and likeness. If you think about it, you will notice that we
usually make him react as we would do if we were in his
place. We find it difficult to believe that the Lord continues to love us infinitely and is waiting for us to make the

least gesture of return so that he can take us in his arms and forgive us as if we had never been separated from him. Rather, we conceive him as being annoyed with us; we think he has had enough of treachery and rejection; we read a frown on his face, he doesn't seem to be very friendly. . . . That is precisely the attitude we would adopt were we in his place. And, no doubt, it influences us when we want to return to him and correct our behavior. Perhaps that is why Saint Bernard said that "we need a mediator near that mediator, and no one can better fill this role than Mary." Do you know why? Because—and this too comes from Saint Bernard—"In her there is nothing austere, nothing awesome. Everything is gentleness." That is just what a man needs when he is wounded, tired, and ill-treated, when he almost can't stand himself.

There is another reason. If you try to think just for a moment about all the serious sins that are committed in the world every day, the tremendous number of times Christ is crucified again, day after day, you will be amazed at God's patience. The salvific will of God, his desire to save men, is quite remarkable—the excuses (I know that is not the right way of putting it, but I can do no better) the excuses he seeks for postponing the hecatomb for which our persistent sinning cries out. But man in his pride finds it very difficult to bow his head. So, it is less humiliating to hang one's head before the Virgin Mary than before Almighty God. All right: God knows us very well, he knows so well the extent to which our nature is wounded by original sin that—if I may put it this way—he gives us an elegant way out by putting us in Mary's presence. No one feels humiliated by having recourse to his mother because, deep down, though maybe very deep down, he is always in some way a child in her presence—and you can find stubbornness in a child, but not pride. And she is our Mother because her Son gave her to us when he was nailed to the Cross: "Behold, your mother," he said, and Saint Augustine points out that "she is the Mother of the members of Christ because she cooperated through her love in the birth, in the Church, of the faithful, who are the members of that Head." She is not a stranger or some troublesome relative or a woman one meets by accident. She is our Mother. Like Saint John, all that we have to do is to receive her as our Mother, recognize her as our Mother, with all the consequences this recognition brings with it.

The first of these consequences probably is that we should be on close terms with her. I mean that if you cannot treat a person as a lifeless object, neither can you regard Mary as your Mother and yet treat her as if she were a piece of furniture. A personal relationship is the first expression of recognition.

I dare say that for most young people this requisite is met by saying a Hail Mary when going to bed and, perhaps, asking her help in an emergency. Personally, I feel that is like treating her as a servant, as someone to whom one says "Good night" out of manners and for whom one rings during the day whenever her services are required. But it's better than nothing.

Then, too, it is fairly clear that everyone has a lot of work to do every day and that it is difficult to find the necessary time and recollection from one end of the day to the other to converse with her, to relate to her. Can you not speak to her with the spontaneity, naturalness, and attention you find in your dealings with your friends or, at home, with your parents?

I don't think so—except for a moment now and then—and only after training. And I don't think even the Church thinks it's easy for most people—to judge by the effort she has been making for centuries to get us to say the Rosary. It's my impression that, given the hustle of life today, our relationship with Mary—a daily, warm, affectionate, and continuous relationship—consists precisely in the Rosary, and that's what she likes most.

For there to be a personal relationship between two people the most important thing is that they have something to say; for a conversation can be turned into something painful when one of them doesn't know what to say or how to put it or one is not interested in knowing what the other wants to say. Well, I don't think this is ever the case as far as our Lady is concerned. You know exactly what you have to say: you should greet her in the way the angel did when he told her about the mystery of the Incarnation; fill her with joy by praising her as the Holy Spirit did through Saint Elizabeth, calling her blessed among women; remind her of her Son, the cause of her joy. And then, humbly, we ought to recognize our destitution by begging her to "pray for us sinners." Not just for me: for us, for all her children. It is a familial rather than a community prayer.

And she likes all this, times over, because, as a mother, she is interested in anything her child says to her, however repetitious it may be, however silly it may sound. So if it's not silly, obviously she's interested in it. And this is useful to us. Twice a week, as we cover the various mysteries of the Rosary, we recall that Jesus was born, suffered, and died for us and is now in heaven and has sent us the Holy Spirit; and these mysteries remind us of what he said to his disciples when he still lived on the earth: "Where I am you may be also" (Jn 14: 3). And then comes the litany, when, once more, after each of her wonderful names, we ask her to pray for us. Anyone who has read Saint Josemaría Escrivá's *Holy Rosary* will know very well what I mean.

It is the easiest way and the best way to keep up a

personal relationship with our Lady—the easiest, because it's within everyone's reach, even children's. You don't have to be very intelligent or very holy or have a great capacity for thinking. It doesn't take up much time. You can say a decade in two minutes, and you don't have to say the whole Rosary at one time (as people used to do, before going to bed or after tea); you can say one mystery now and one some other time; you can learn how to make use of short bus journeys and so forth and have the whole Rosary said by mid-afternoon. The net result is that you will have remembered her affectionately at different times of the day. And don't tell me you get distracted; if you take that approach you would have to give up studying—because you get distracted then, too—and attending lectures also, of course.

I was saying that I have the impression that of all the means available to us for keeping daily contact with Mary, the Rosary is the best one because it is the one she herself most likes. Fortunately, I don't have to be very clever to show that.

In 1917, something remarkable happened in Fatima, in Portugal. Our Lady appeared to three village children, and they were sufficiently children and sufficiently unsophisticated to allow you to dismiss, at the outset, any idea of invention, fraud, or sick joke. The whole thing was spread over a number of months: it was quite public; everyone knew about it. It took place at a time when rationalist criticism and prejudice against any kind of supernatural manifestation were so widespread that fraud was practically impossible; and it occurred in so anti-clerical an environment that jeers, derision, and difficulties provided the setting of the whole affair. Given all these filters and the testimony of thousands of people and many newspapers, it is a well-documented fact, from the historical point of view.

I should make it clear that it is not a thing you have to believe in. God's revelation to men—the official revelation, I mean, which the Church has the job of keeping and passing on—was closed with the death of the last witness of the Resurrection, who was an apostle. And only the truths contained in that revelation are proposed to us by the Church as something we have an obligation firmly to hold. What our Lady communicated to the children at Fatima, as also what she said seventy years before to Bernadette in Lourdes, falls into the category of "private revelation." Therefore, it is not something that God reveals officially to the world as necessary for salvation because, as I have just said, that was all said and done when the last apostle died. Rather, it is a sort of private, unofficial message or notification—something designed to help our innate weakness. And it is up to the Church to say, in each case, whether such and such a private apparition or revelation is legitimate, that is, whether it carries the hallmark of the divine. If the Church pronounces in favor (as in the case of Fatima and Lourdes), this means that any Catholic may believe in it without danger (indeed, with benefit) to his faith, but he is not obliged to believe in it.

Anyway, when the children of Fatima asked the Lady who she was, she replied in these words: "*A Senhora do Rosano*"—Our Lady of the Rosary. (To Bernadette she had said: "I am the Immaculate Conception.") To define herself as Our Lady of the Rosary is, to use today's jargon, really committing herself. And she was carrying rosary beads, and often implored the children to say the Rosary and to get others to say it. Indeed, in Lourdes she almost prayed it herself. I say "almost' because she had a Rosary there, too, and I read somewhere that she recited the beads, and, although she did not move her lips as Bernadette was saying the Hail Marys, she did so in reply to the Glory at the end of each mystery. I think that that indicates she likes the Rosary.

I suppose you haven't read a book by Lope de Vega called *The Devout Practice of the Rosary*.* He says many beautiful things praising this expression of a child's love (for that is what the Rosary is):

> This is a prayer which I each day pray to the Virgin, and which I would like you to pray too: for in divine heavenly ways she will give you freedom with hope, which she can obtain from her Son in unlimited amounts.

That is what he says: she will give us freedom with hope. Not a freedom like that which, for example, a certain existentialist school promotes, a freedom without purpose or content, whose only way out is suicide, a freedom without hope. And not a hope without freedom, such as Marxists preach as the only way out of slavery, on an oppressive and absolutely closed horizon, when there is nothing, nothing, that one can choose, for all choice is prohibited, for no choice is possible. A freedom with hope: that is the freedom Christ has gained for us and that his Mother hands us.

God's tenderness toward men—that is what Mary is. That is why Saint Bernard could say: "You will not go astray if you follow her, you will not despair if you pray to her, you will not get lost if you think about her. If she gives you her hand, you will not fall; if she protects you, you will have nothing to fear; you will not grow tired if she is your guide; you will arrive safely home if she helps you."

Do you think the Rosary is too high a price to pay for all that?

---

* Lope de Vega, *La devocion del Rosario* (Madrid: Biblioteca de Autores Cristianos, 1968).